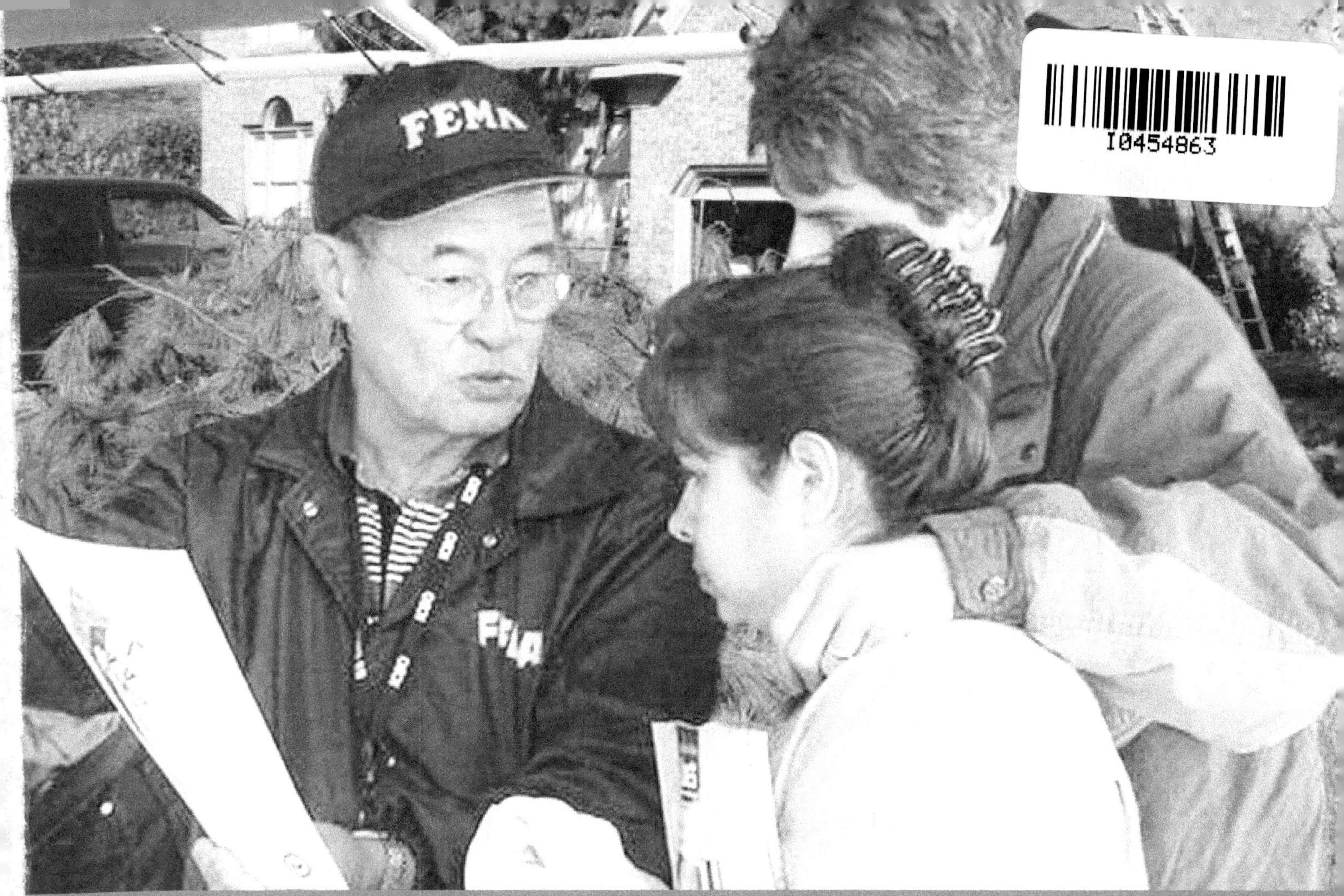

Protecting Your Home or Small Business From Disasters

IS-394.A

December 2005

FEMA

TABLE OF CONTENTS

Lesson 1. Overview: Protecting Against Disasters

Lesson 2. Protecting Against Water Damage

Lesson 3. Protecting Against Wind Damage

TABLE OF CONTENTS (Continued)

Lesson 3. Protecting Against Wind Damage (Continued)

Lesson 4. Protecting Against Wildfires

Lesson 5. Protecting Against Earthquake Damage

Federal Emergency Management Agency Training

The Federal Emergency Management Agency (FEMA) is the central point of contact within the Federal Government for a wide range of emergency management activities. The agency has numerous roles, including coordinating Government activities, providing planning assistance, guiding and advising various agencies, and delivering training.

FEMA's training program is delivered through the Emergency Management Institute (EMI). EMI provides emergency management training to enhance emergency management practices throughout the United States for the full range of potential emergencies.

A complete listing of EMI courses is available on FEMA's website. The address is http://www.fema.gov.

Independent Study Courses

FEMA's independent study program is one of the ways that emergency management training is provided to the general public and to emergency management audiences. Many independent study courses are available through FEMA's website. All courses are suitable for either individual or group enrollment and are available at no charge.

Protecting Your Home or Small Business From Disasters

A constant stream of news stories remind us that disasters can disrupt our lives and damage our homes and businesses with little or no notice.

This independent study course will address different types of hazards and describe specific measures that you can take to protect your home or place of business. No prior knowledge of the subject is assumed. This course will provide a foundation of knowledge that will enable you to:

- Explain how protective measures can reduce or eliminate long-term risks to your home and personal property from hazards and their effects.
- Explain how protective measures for small businesses secure people, business property, and building structures and prevent business loss following a natural disaster.
- Describe different types of natural disasters.
- Describe hazards that pose a risk to your home or small business.

Course Lessons

This course has five lessons:

Lesson 1. Overview: Protecting Against Disasters—Provides an overview of the types of disasters that are most likely to damage homes and businesses, and addresses the likelihood that these hazards will affect your community.

Lesson 2. Protecting Against Water Damage—Describes how to determine your risk of flooding, describes a range of methods to avoid water damage, and discusses the National Flood Insurance Program (NFIP).

Lesson 3. Protecting Against Wind Damage—Describes risks from hurricanes and tornadoes, and provides methods to protect your home or place of business from wind damage.

Lesson 4. Protecting Against Wildfires—Describes locations that are particularly susceptible to damage from wildfires, and actions you can take to protect your home or place of business from wildfires.

Lesson 5. Protecting Against Earthquake Damage—Discusses areas of the United States that are considered most at risk from earthquakes, and describes ways to protect your home or place of business from earthquake damage.

How To Complete the Course

You may complete this course at your own pace. Definitions of important terms used throughout the course appear in the Glossary located after Lesson 5.

A short quiz follows each lesson. Use the Answer Key located after the Glossary to check your answers. If you have missed any questions, go back and review the material again.

As an option, credit can be provided to those who successfully complete the entire course and score at least 75 percent on a final examination. To take the final examination, log on to http://training.fema.gov/EMIWeb/IS/ and follow the links for *Protecting Your Home or Small Business From Disasters, IS 394.A.* Those who pass the examination can expect to receive a certificate of completion within 2 weeks from the date the examination is received at FEMA.

Questions about this option should be directed to the FEMA Independent Study Program by calling 1-800-238-2258 and asking for the Independent Study Office or emailing at independent.study@dhs.gov.

Lesson 1. Overview: Protecting Against Disasters

Emergencies and natural disasters can occur anywhere in the United States. Televised scenes of flooded homes or buildings scattered like matchsticks in the wake of a tornado or hurricane remind us that our own homes and businesses could be vulnerable.

Americans face more severe weather than citizens of any other country. National Weather Service figures indicate that in an average year, the United States experiences:

- 2,500 floods.
- 1,000 tornadoes.
- 10 hurricanes.

Severe weather is only one source of disaster. Earthquakes and wildfires also may threaten your home or place of business with damage or destruction. The Federal Emergency Management Agency (FEMA) estimates that as much as 75 percent of the Nation's housing could be at risk from natural hazards.

Self-Assessment Questions:

- Has your current home and/or place of business been affected by an emergency or disaster since you lived or did business in this location?

  __ Yes   __ No

- To your knowledge, was your community affected by a disaster during the last 10 years?

  __ Yes   __ No

- To your knowledge, is your community considered at risk for one or more kinds of disasters?

  __ Yes   __ No

Lesson 1. Overview: Protecting Against Disasters

As you plan to protect your home or place of business from disaster, think about the kind of natural hazards you are most likely to face.

In this course, you will learn about protecting against:

- Water damage due to flooding, the most common type of disaster.
- Wind damage from hurricanes and tornadoes.
- Wildfires in forested and rural areas.
- Earthquakes.

The course focuses on hazards for which you can take measures to protect your home or business. Disasters such as volcanic eruptions, tsunamis, and landslides give few options other than ensuring the safety of your family and/or employees.

Self-Assessment Questions:

- Check below the type of hazard that you believe most threatens your home or place of business.

    __ Flooding   __ Hurricane   __ Tornado   __ Wildfire   __ Earthquake

- Other hazards likely to affect your area are _____

    _____ and _____
    (Complete only if applicable.)

Ask your local government officials for information about the specific hazards that pose the greatest risks in your area. Building and zoning officials, planning departments, floodplain managers, or emergency managers should be familiar with your community's history and can tell you about local plans and programs aimed at helping you protect your home or place of business.

Protective Measures

The lesson for each type of hazard will describe:

- Nonstructural, generally low-cost measures you can take.

  An example of a nonstructural measure: Clearing brush and vegetation around buildings to prevent wildfire damage.

- Structural measures that involve changes to the building.

  Examples of structural measures: Elevating a flood-prone building or, in an area subject to earthquakes, bolting the bottom of the structure to the foundation.

Success Stories

There are many examples of how protective measures have benefited owners of homes and businesses when disaster struck. Here are two, one for a home and one for a business.

Homeowners: South Portland, Maine

The City of South Portland has an old combined sewer system. When it rains, all of the runoff goes into the system. When heavy rain and flooding occur, the sewer system is overwhelmed and the cellars of houses are swamped. This has resulted in health hazards and repeated damage to items in the basements.

Homeowners with backflow problems called David Thomas, Collection Systems Manager for the City of South Portland, who got the idea to have backflow preventers installed in homes with such problems.

In February 1998, the City began its Backwater Valve Program and installed valves in 89 participating houses within 5 months. Each valve cost $397, including installation.

The program is considered a success. Despite a June 1998 rainfall of more than 10 inches that caused flooding across central and southern Maine, none of the participating homeowners reported flooding. Since the valves were installed, the City has not received any calls from distressed homeowners.

Savings in avoided damages from the 1998 flood and future floods is expected to be at least $75,000.

Business: Fort Myers Beach, Florida

When Hurricane Charley hit Fort Myers Beach in August 2004, four buildings at Tom Kolar's Lighthouse Resort Inn and Suites, which sits 200 feet from the beach at San Carlos Bay, remained dry, undamaged, and full of customers. Other hotels and motels on the island were damaged or flooded, and closed.

In the past, the Lighthouse Resort would have been closed, too. In two decades there have been seven hurricane events causing flood and wind-related damage to the Resort, leaving the third-generation owner to deal with nearly $100,000 in repair costs per event. When Charley hit, the four undamaged buildings remained high and dry, having been elevated as part of a joint State, Federal, and local mitigation project. In approximately one year the savings on repair costs alone totaled nearly $200,000, almost 50% of the mitigation investment.

"Everybody else was out of business but he (Kolar) was renting rooms," said Bob Rockwell, the local contractor who worked on the recent mitigation project. He had worked on many of the previous repairs, and spurred the project after he spotted a television program in 2001 about the Federal Emergency Management Agency (FEMA) Flood Mitigation Assistance (FMA) program.

Working with Ft. Myers Beach Deputy Town Manager, John Gucciardo, Kolar and Rockwell got the ball rolling and gained the necessary approvals for the jointly funded mitigation project to elevate six of the Resort's buildings. Hoping to prevent future repetitive losses and the subsequent effects not only for the owner but also on the community, work was begun in March of 2003, and two more buildings are scheduled to be elevated by year's end. The project's aim is to elevate the six repetitive loss structures 2 feet above the projected flood level, but the owner exceeded the goal by several additional feet.

If there was a "silver lining" in the clouds of hurricanes Charley and Frances, it is that they have now demonstrated the value of the Lighthouse Resort Inn and Suites mitigation project. For the owner, the repetitive losses, ever-increasing repair costs, and lost income will be avoided. Employees will avoid the anxiety of losing their income due to time lost for lengthy repairs. The town and State will recognize tax benefits from the increased value and extended life of the mitigated property. For the National Flood Insurance Program, it means reduced or eliminated repetitive payments for damage claims.

"Adjacent property owners benefit," said Gucciardo, "because the project is located in a Community Redevelopment Area and the additional tax revenue must be invested back into the local area." According to Gucciardo, the town is even seeing benefits such as no expenditure for debris removal, a staggering post-hurricane task for the area. "Other properties did not fare as well (as the Resort)," he stated, "and we expect to be dealing with debris removal for weeks to come."

As a result of undertaking the joint investment in the mitigation, the Lighthouse Resort is "open for business," a welcome oasis in the midst of so much destruction. "Mr. Kolar is very pleased, very happy, especially after the hurricane, and I'm thrilled," Rockwell stated.

Lesson 1. Overview: Protecting Against Disasters

The questions below review key points in protecting against disasters. After completing the questions, you can check your answers on the answer sheet located after the course glossary.

1. The most common type of disaster in the United States is

   _____.

2. This course will cover the following types of hazards that threaten your home or place of business. (Mark all that apply.)

   ☐ Flooding

   ☐ Landslide

   ☐ Earthquake

   ☐ Tornado

   ☐ Hurricane

   ☐ Tsunami

   ☐ Wildfire

3. Write below two sources of local government information you can consult to learn about hazards that affect your area.

   _____

   _____

4. An example of a structural measure to protect against damage is to elevate a building in a flood-prone area.

   _____ True   _____ False

Introduction

Floods can happen in cities, in mountains, and in deserts. Every year, more homes and businesses are damaged by floods than by any other natural disaster. Floods move, and can spread for miles. Strong currents can sweep away the belongings of a lifetime and leave behind a thick layer of mud and debris.

Your home or business can be flooded even if you don't live near water. Storms, melting snow, dam and levee failure, or drainage system failure can occur far from a river, lake, or ocean. Hurricanes often generate torrential rains for hundreds of miles inland. If your community is located near a river, lake, or coastline, the chances increase that your home or place of business will suffer damage from flooded rivers, waves, and storm surges.

How Great Is Your Risk of Flooding?

Self-Assessment Questions:

- Has your current home and/or place of business been affected by flooding since you lived or did business in this location?

  __ Yes   __ No

- To your knowledge, was your community affected by flooding during the last 10 years?

  __ Yes   __ No

Check with your local floodplain manager, building official, city engineer, or planning and zoning administrator. They can tell you whether you live or have a business located in a Special Flood Hazard Area.

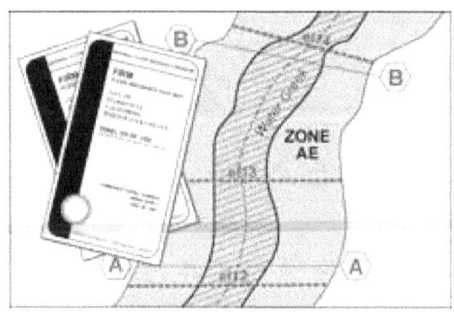

Figure 1. Graphic Showing a Portion of a Flood Map

Ask to see a flood map of your community, which may show a projected flood level for your neighborhood or place of business.

If you know how high floodwaters might reach, you have an idea how much water could come in.

Protecting Personal Property

If your home or place of business has a basement or lower level, think about what would happen if water enters the space. Move possessions to a higher floor as appropriate for your situation. Take photos or videos of important possessions for insurance purposes.

Make sure that items such as important documents and irreplaceable personal objects such as photographs are stored in a safe location, if possible in watertight containers.

If major flooding is expected:

- Bring in outdoor furniture and other personal property kept outdoors.
- Secure outbuildings.
- Consider putting your valuables in a storage facility in a safe, nonflooding location.

Retrofitting Your House or Place of Business

Retrofitting is making changes to an existing building to protect it from flooding or other hazards such as high winds and earthquakes.

If you decide to retrofit your house or place of business, you'll need to be aware of other potential hazards such as high winds and earthquakes.

Retrofitting may range from simple measures you can perform yourself to major construction. Retrofitting includes:

- Measures to protect utilities and service equipment.
- Dry floodproofing to protect against shallow flooding.
- Elevating the structure above the projected flood level.
- Relocating the structure away from the flood hazard area.

FEMA and other Federal agencies offer a wide array of assistance programs that help States, communities, and individual property owners protect against the negative effects of flood hazards.

You may be eligible to receive financial assistance through one or more flood protection programs that will help pay for your retrofitting project. Check with your local officials, your NFIP State Coordinator, or the FEMA Regional Office for your State.

A professional contractor licensed to work in your State, county, or city should make changes that:

- Are complicated or large-scale.
- Affect the structure of your house or place of business.
- Affect electrical wiring and plumbing.

Check with your local building department about building permit requirements. Make sure that changes meet local building code standards.

Protecting Utilities and Service Equipment

During a flood, equipment such as furnaces, water heaters, and electrical meters may be inundated and ruined. Sewer backups present another costly and unpleasant possibility. Protecting utilities and equipment from flood damage can involve changes that vary in complexity and cost.

The measures you take depend on whether key utilities and equipment are exposed to flood damage in current locations. Possible actions are to:

- Raise or floodproof heating, ventilation, and cooling (HVAC) equipment.
- Raise the main electric switch box, electric outlets, switches, light sockets, baseboard heaters, and wiring.
- Elevate the washer and dryer.
- Anchor fuel tanks.

To protect against drainage system backups, you can install:

- A floating floor drain plug.
- A sewage system backflow valve.

Protecting HVAC Equipment

In flood-prone buildings, a good way to protect HVAC equipment is to move it from the basement or lower level to an upper floor, or even to the attic. A less desirable method is to build a concrete or masonry block floodwall around the equipment. Relocation can involve plumbing and electrical changes, and floodwalls must be adequately designed and constructed to be strong and high enough to provide the protection needed.

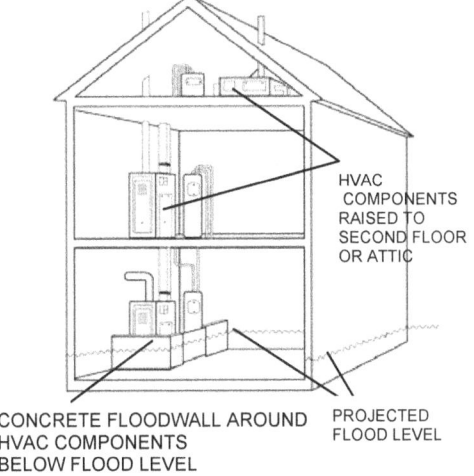

CONCRETE FLOODWALL AROUND HVAC COMPONENTS BELOW FLOOD LEVEL

PROJECTED FLOOD LEVEL

HVAC COMPONENTS RAISED TO SECOND FLOOR OR ATTIC

Figure 2. Graphic Showing HVAC Protection Methods

If you are having your existing furnace or hot water heater repaired or replaced, consider having it relocated at the same time. It probably will be cheaper to combine projects than to do them separately. If you decide to raise your HVAC equipment, consider upgrading to a more energy-efficient unit at the same time. Upgrading not only can save you money on your heating and cooling bills, but also may make you eligible for a rebate from your utility company. If you decide to protect your HVAC equipment with a floodwall, remember to leave enough space in the enclosed area for repairs and maintenance. If the wall has an opening to provide access to the enclosed area, the opening will need to have a gate that can be closed to prevent floodwaters from entering.

Protecting Utilities and Service Equipment (Continued)

Protecting Electrical Systems

Electrical system components, including service panels (fuse and circuit breaker boxes), meters, switches, and outlets, are easily damaged by floodwater. If inundated even for short periods, components probably will have to be replaced. Another concern is the potential for fire caused by short circuits in flooded systems. Raising electrical system components helps you avoid damage. After a flood, an undamaged, operating electrical system will help you clean up, make repairs, and move back into your home or business with fewer delays.

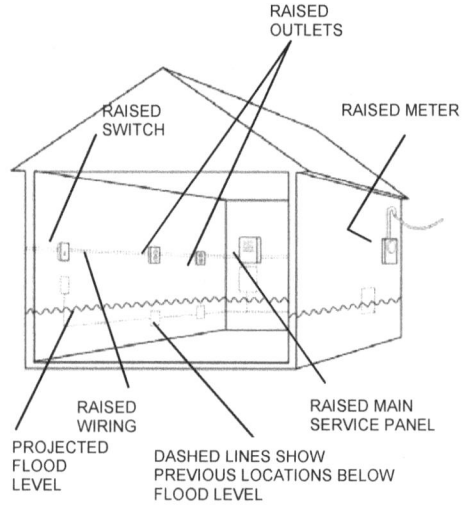

Figure 3. Graphic Illustrating Methods for Protecting Electrical Systems

All components of the electrical system, including the wiring, should be raised at least 1 foot above the base flood level for your location.

Your contractor should check with the local power company about the maximum height that the electric meter can be raised.

If your house or place of business is equipped with an old-style fuse box or low-amperage service, you may want to consider upgrading to a modern circuit breaker system and higher amperage service, especially if you have large appliances or other electrical equipment that draw a lot of power.

Protecting Your Washer and Dryer

Your washer and dryer may be elevated on masonry or pressure-treated lumber at least 1 foot above the projected flood level.

Protecting Utilities and Service Equipment (Continued)

Anchoring Fuel Tanks

Unanchored fuel tanks can be easily moved by floodwaters, and cause serious threats to you, your family, and your home or business.

When floodwaters move an unanchored fuel tank in your basement, the supply line can tear free and your basement can be contaminated by oil.

An unanchored fuel tank outside your house or place of business can be driven into walls and swept downstream to damage other houses and buildings. Propane is stored in pressurized vessels as liquefied petroleum gas (LPG), which can be extremely volatile and potentially explosive if the tank is ruptured and a spark ignites the escaping LPG.

Even a buried tank can be pushed to the surface by the buoyant effect of soil saturated by water.

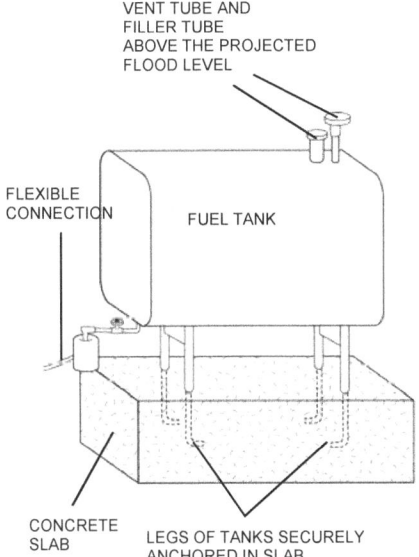

VENT TUBE AND
FILLER TUBE
ABOVE THE PROJECTED
FLOOD LEVEL

FLEXIBLE
CONNECTION

FUEL TANK

CONCRETE
SLAB

LEGS OF TANKS SECURELY
ANCHORED IN SLAB

**Figure 4. Graphic Showing an
Anchored Fuel Tank**

One way to anchor a tank is to attach it to a large concrete slab heavy enough to resist the force of floodwaters.

This method can be used for all tanks, both inside and outside your house or place of business.

You can also anchor an outside tank by running straps over it and attaching the straps to ground anchors.

Ground anchors and straps are the same products required by building codes to tie down mobile homes. Anchors and straps are available from suppliers and installers that service the manufactured home industry.

Protecting Utilities and Service Equipment (Continued)

Protecting Against Drain and Sewer Backups

A sump pump with backup power is a key tool to prevent ground water from entering a building.

If you have a floor drain, you can install a floating floor drain plug at the current drain location. If the floor drainpipe backs up, the float will rise and plug the drain.

In some floodprone areas, flooding can cause sewage from sanitary sewer lines to back up into houses through drainpipes. These backups not only cause damage that is difficult to repair, but also create health hazards.

A good way to protect your house from sewage backups is to install backflow valves, which are designed to block drainpipes temporarily and prevent flow into the house. Backflow valves are available in a variety of designs that range from the simple to the complex.

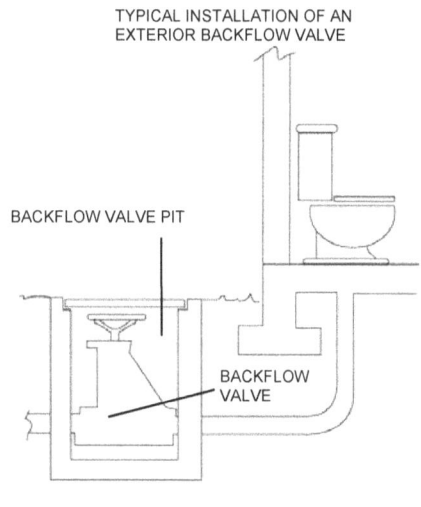

TYPICAL INSTALLATION OF AN
EXTERIOR BACKFLOW VALVE

BACKFLOW VALVE PIT

BACKFLOW
VALVE

← NORMAL DIRECTION OF FLOW (VALVE
PREVENTS FLOW IN REVERSE DIRECTION)

Figure 5. Graphic Showing a Gate Valve

The illustration shows a gate valve, one of the more complex designs. It provides a strong seal, but must be operated by hand. The effectiveness of a gate valve will depend on how much warning you have of impending flooding. Simpler valves include flap or check valves, which open to allow flow out of the house but close when the flow reverses. These valves operate automatically, but do not provide as strong a seal as a gate valve.

Some valves combine the advantages of flap and gate valves in a single design. Your plumber or contractor can advise you of the relative advantages and disadvantages of different types of backflow valves.

If you have a sump pump, it may be connected to underground drain lines that may be difficult to seal off.

Making Major Structural Changes

Flood protection measures that involve major structural changes are:

- Dry floodproofing.
- Elevating your house or building(s) used for your business.
- Relocating structures above projected flood levels.

Dry Floodproofing

Even in areas where floodwaters are less than 2 feet deep, a building can be severely damaged if water reaches the interior. Damage to walls and floors can be expensive to repair, and the building may be unusable while repairs are underway.

One way to protect a house or place of business from shallow flooding is to add a waterproof veneer to the exterior walls and seal all openings, including doors, to prevent water from entering. This approach is called "dry floodproofing."

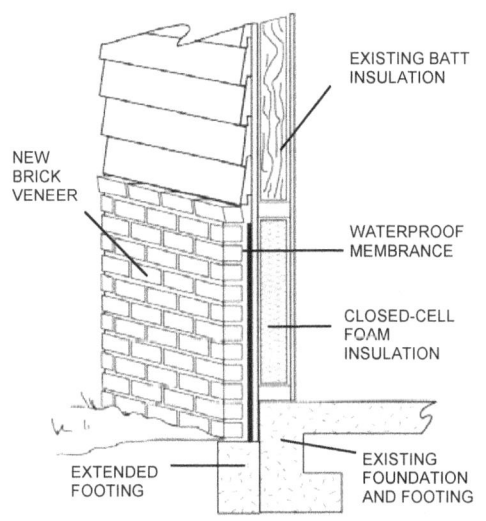

NEW BRICK VENEER

EXISTING BATT INSULATION

WATERPROOF MEMBRANCE

CLOSED-CELL FOAM INSULATION

EXTENDED FOOTING

EXISTING FOUNDATION AND FOOTING

Figure 6. Graphic Showing Application of Waterproof Veneer

The veneer can be a layer of brick backed by a waterproof membrane. Before the veneer is applied, the siding is removed and replaced with exterior grade plywood sheathing. If necessary, the existing foundation footing is extended to support the brick. If the building has brick walls, the new brick veneer and waterproof membrane are added over the existing brick.

Because the wall will be exposed to floodwater, changes are made to the interior walls as well so that they will resist moisture damage.

In the area below the projected flood level, standard batt insulation is replaced with washable closed-cell foam insulation, and any wood blocking added inside the wall cavity is made of exterior grade lumber.

In a building that is dry floodproofed, all openings below the projected flood level must be sealed, including not only doors and windows but also the openings for water pipes, gas and electric lines, dryer vents, and sump pump discharge pipes.

Making Major Structural Changes (Continued)

Dry Floodproofing (Continued)

If your house or place of business is being remodeled or repaired, consider having the veneer added as part of the remodeling or repair work.

When flood depths exceed 2 feet, the pressure on waterproofed walls increases greatly, usually beyond the strength of the walls. Dry floodproofing is not appropriate if greater depths are expected. Also, if flooding comes from ground water entering through the floor, dry floodproofing will not be effective.

Dry floodproofing:

- Does not reduce flood insurance premiums for homes.
- When flooding threatens, makes you responsible for installing flood shields on openings in time to keep water from entering.

Elevation

Elevating a house to prevent floodwaters from reaching living areas is an effective retrofitting method. The goal of the elevation process is to raise the lowest floor to or above the projected flood level.

Figure 7. Graphic Showing an Elevated House

You can elevate the entire house, including the floor, or leave the house in its existing position and construct a new, elevated floor within the house. The method used depends largely on construction type, foundation type, and flooding conditions.

During the elevation process, most houses (including manufactured homes) are separated from their foundations, raised on hydraulic jacks, and held by temporary supports while a new or extended foundation is constructed below.

Making Major Structural Changes (Continued)

Elevation (Continued)

Elevation works well for houses originally built on basement, crawlspace, and open foundations. As explained later in this section, the new or extended foundation can consist of continuous walls or separate piers, posts, columns, or pilings.

A variation of elevation is used for houses on slab-on-grade foundations. In these houses, the slab forms both the foundation and the floor of the house. Elevating these houses is easier if the house is left attached to the slab foundation and both are lifted together. After the house and slab are lifted, a new foundation is constructed below the slab.

Alternative techniques are available for masonry houses on slab-on-grade foundations. These techniques do not require the lifting of the house. Instead, they involve raising the floor within the house or moving the living space to an upper story.

Although elevating a building can help protect it from floodwaters, you need to consider other hazards such as wind and earthquakes before choosing this method.

Making Major Structural Changes (Continued)

Relocation

Relocation—moving your house or place of business out of the flood hazard area—offers the greatest protection from flooding. It also can free you from anxiety about future floods and lower or even eliminate your insurance premiums. However, relocation usually is the most expensive of the retrofitting methods.

The relocation process involves lifting a house or other building off its foundation, placing it on a heavy-duty flatbed trailer, hauling it to a new site outside the flood hazard area, and lowering it onto a new, conventional foundation. The process sounds straightforward, but a number of considerations require careful planning.

A building must be structurally sound to be picked up and moved successfully. All the structural members and their connections must be able to withstand the stresses imposed when the building is lifted and moved. Before the building is lifted, the moving contractor must inspect it to verify its structural soundness. A house or other building that is in poor condition, especially one that has been damaged by flooding, may need so much structural repair and bracing that relocation will not be practical.

Relocation is sometimes used as an alternative to demolition when a house has been damaged. Instead of demolishing the house, the owner may be able to sell it for salvage to a contractor, who will then move the house to another site, renovate it, and sell it. Relocation can also occur after a community acquires a floodprone property from the owner. Rather than leaving the house to be demolished, the owner may decide to keep the house and move it to property outside the flood hazard area.

For information about house relocation companies, contact the International Association of Structural Movers (ISM) at P.O. Box 1213, Elbridge, NY 13060, (315) 689-9498.

Flood Insurance

If you own a structure in a flood hazard area and you obtained a mortgage or loan to build, buy, or remodel that structure, your lender had to make sure you were covered by flood insurance. It's a Federal law.

Self-Assessment Question:

Do you currently have a flood insurance policy for your home and/or place of business?

___ Yes   ___ No

Flood insurance is available to residents in more than 19,000 communities across the United States that participate in the National Flood Insurance Program (NFIP).

Most homeowners insurance doesn't cover damage to structures and contents from flooding, flood-related erosion, and flood-caused mudslides. Flood insurance does.

Federal law requires flood insurance in an amount equal to the outstanding principal balance on your mortgage or loan, the value of the building, or the maximum limit of coverage available, whichever is least.

While the law only requires coverage for the loan balance, consider protecting your equity as well. Up to $250,000 in coverage is available for single-family residential buildings and $100,000 is available for contents.

Up to $1 million in coverage is available for your business, $500,000 to cover the buildings and $500,000 to cover the contents.

You can buy flood insurance even if you don't live or own a business in a flood hazard area. Approximately one in four flood insurance claims comes from areas where the flood risk is rated low or moderate.

Check into the low-cost Preferred Risk Policy, which offers coverage in low and moderate risk areas.

It takes 30 days for a flood policy to take effect, so you need to purchase flood insurance before flooding happens.

For more information about flood insurance, call:

1-888-CALL FLOOD or TDD# 1-800-427-5593 (toll-free telephone numbers)

Flood Insurance Resources

Resources on the NFIP at the FEMA website
(www.fema.gov/library/prepandprev.shtm#mit) include:

- Answers to Questions About the NFIP
- Avoiding Flood Damage: A Checklist for Homeowners
- Coping With a Flood - Before, During & After
- Flood: Are You Protected From the Next Disaster?
- How the NFIP Works
- How You Can Benefit From the New ICC Endorsement
- Myths & Facts
- Nothing Could Dampen the Joy of Home Ownership
- Preferred Risk Policy
- Things You Should Know About Flood Insurance
- Tips on Handling Your Flood Insurance Claim
- Top 10 Facts Every Consumer Needs To Know About the NFIP
- What You Need To Know About Federal Disaster Assistance & National Flood Insurance
- Who Is at Risk for Flooding?
- Why You Should Have a Preferred Risk Policy
- Your Homeowners Insurance Doesn't Cover Floods
- National Flood Insurance Program (NFIP) Program Description

Success Stories

Skagit County, Washington

When a property owner built a rental home, he elevated it a little higher than county regulations demanded.

Acting as a general contractor, the owner elevated the house as county regulations instructed. The 100-year flood level is gauged at 43 feet, and the county insists that new homes be elevated to 44 feet, one foot above flood stage.

The owner took no chances; he elevated the house to 45 feet, and it was a good investment. When flooding came to Skagit County in October 2002, the home was a safe 5 feet above the floodwaters. "My renter has a dry home, and my rental income is uninterrupted," he said. "Elevation worked as advertised."

The renter was displaced for a couple of days, but there were no property losses associated with the flood. "Just a little washing after the water receded," the owner said. "I'm delighted, and so is my renter." By elevating, the owner saved his investment and his renter's personal property.

Success Stories (Continued)

Santa Barbara, California

On the morning of January 10, 1995, the staff of the United Way arrived at their facility in downtown Santa Barbara to find 3 feet of water in their offices. Flooding destroyed computers, carpet, furniture, workstation partitions, electrical wiring, and irreplaceable documents. Elevators, the alarm system, cabinets, and interior walls were also damaged.

Flooding in the city was the result of 7 hours of heavy rainfall the night before that generated runoff from the nearby hills, plus an unusually high tide that overwhelmed the city's pumping systems and fill culverts.

Everything that was destroyed or damaged had to be replaced before operations at United Way could return to normal. Included in the overall loss was the cost of business interruption, emotional impact on staff members, and the effects on United Way's customers during the several months it took to restore operations.

To protect its property from future disasters, United Way developed and implemented a plan to floodproof its building.

Measures taken included installation of three flood control panels (doors) that can be activated to prevent water from coming into the building and reaching the 3-foot level sustained in the 1995 flood. A 2-foot-deep trench was dug around the building foundation and filled with sealant to waterproof the structure. Water-resistant walls, doors, cabinets, and carpeting that can be removed one square at a time were installed. Critical infrastructure including electrical outlets, electrical panels, and the alarm system were elevated.

The cost of repairs of damage from the 1995 flood was $450,000. This sum included the cost of repairing or replacing electrical systems, elevator and alarm systems, computers, carpet, cabinets, doors, furniture and interior walls. The cost of protective measures, including installation of flood doors, the trench and sealant, and elevation of critical lifelines, was $100,000.

What's Best for Your Home or Business?

The protective measures you consider depend on where your house or business is located.

Is your location within a flood hazard area? If so:

- Assess your vulnerability to water damage to the building and to your possessions.
- Decide which protective measures make the most sense in your situation.

Is your location at low or moderate risk of flooding? If so:

- Remember that approximately one in four flood insurance claims comes from areas outside of the flood hazard area.
- Consider buying a low-cost Preferred Risk Policy, which offers coverage in low- and moderate-risk areas.

Flood Protection Resources

A number of publications offer indepth information that can help you learn more about particular flood protection options.

The resources below can be located on the FEMA website (www.fema.gov/library/prepandprev.shtm#mit).

- Above the Flood: Elevating Your Floodprone House
- Addressing Your Community's Flood Problems
- After a Flood: The First Steps
- A Report - Mitigation of Flood and Erosion Damage to Residential Buildings in Coastal Areas
- Coastal Construction Manual: Principles and Practices of Planning, Siting, Designing, Constructing, and Maintaining Residential Buildings in Coastal Areas
- Crawlspace Construction for Buildings Located in Special Flood Hazard Areas
- Design and Construction Guidance for Breakaway Walls Below Elevated Coastal Buildings
- Design Guidelines for Flood Damage Reduction
- Engineering Principles and Practices of Retrofitting Floodprone Residential Structures
- Elevated Residential Structures
- Ensuring that Structures Built on Fill In or Near Special Flood Hazard Areas are Reasonably Safe From Flooding
- Federal Programs Offering Non-structural Flood Recovery and Floodplain Management Alternatives
- Floodproofing Non-Residential Structures
- Flood-Resistant Materials Requirements
- Free-of-Obstruction Requirements
- Hazard Mitigation Grant Program Desk Reference
- Homeowner's Guide to Retrofitting: Six Ways to Protect Your House from Flooding
- Manufactured Home Installation in Flood Hazard Areas
- Non-Residential Floodproofing -- Requirements and Certification
- Openings in Foundation Walls
- Protecting Building Utilities from Flood Damage
- Protecting Building Utilities from Flood Damage: Principles and Practices for Design and Construction of Flood Resistant Utility Systems.
- Repairing Your Flooded Home
- Wet Floodproofing Requirements

Lesson 2. Protecting Against Water Damage

This lesson reviewed the following steps you can take to protect your home or place of business against water damage.

☐ Know your flood risk. Your local building or floodplain management department may be able to provide the projected flood level.

☐ Move important possessions and valuables out of the basement or lower level and store them in safe locations.

☐ Move or elevate any of the following utilities and equipment that are not located above the projected flood level:

- Main electric switch box
- Electric outlets and switches
- Washer and dryer
- Furnace and water heater

☐ Take further protective steps as needed:

- Anchor fuel tanks.
- Install a sump pump with backup power.
- Put float plugs in floor drains.
- Install backflow valves in sewer systems.

☐ As you assess your degree of risk, consider major structural changes, including:

- Dry floodproofing for shallow flooding, especially for nonresidential buildings.
- Elevation.
- Relocation.

☐ Get enough flood insurance to cover potential losses.

Lesson 2. Protecting Against Water Damage

The questions below review key points in protecting against water damage. After completing the questions, you can check your answers on the answer sheet located after the course glossary.

1. A _____ of your community may show a projected flood level for your neighborhood or place of business.

2. Retrofitting measures to protect a structure against water damage include: (Mark all that apply)

   ☐ Elevating utilities and service equipment.

   ☐ Dry floodproofing.

   ☐ Obtaining adequate flood insurance.

   ☐ Elevating the structure above the projected flood level.

3. Write below two utilities that could be moved or elevated above the projected flood level.

   _____

   _____

4. Select the protective measure on the right that would be used to protect the item on the left, and write the appropriate letter on each blank space.

   ___ Floor drains   a. Install backflow valves

   ___ Sewer system   b. Anchor

   ___ Fuel tanks   c. Elevate

   ___ Washer and dryer   d. Install float plugs

5. You can buy flood insurance even if you don't live or own a business in a flood hazard area.

   ___ True   ___ False

Lesson 3. Protecting Against Wind Damage

Wind can tear the roofs from buildings, rip siding from exterior walls, and throw debris through windows. Falling trees can crush roofs and walls.

Of course, hurricanes and tornadoes generate exceptionally destructive winds that can turn buildings into piles of rubble. But high winds can happen anywhere, and strike during many types of storms.

Self-Assessment Question: How much warning do you have to protect against wind damage?

Hurricane watches and warnings usually provide 2 or 3 days' notice to protect your home or business and evacuate, if necessary.

Tornadoes, on the other hand, strike with little warning. Ensuring the safety of your family and employees becomes a top priority.

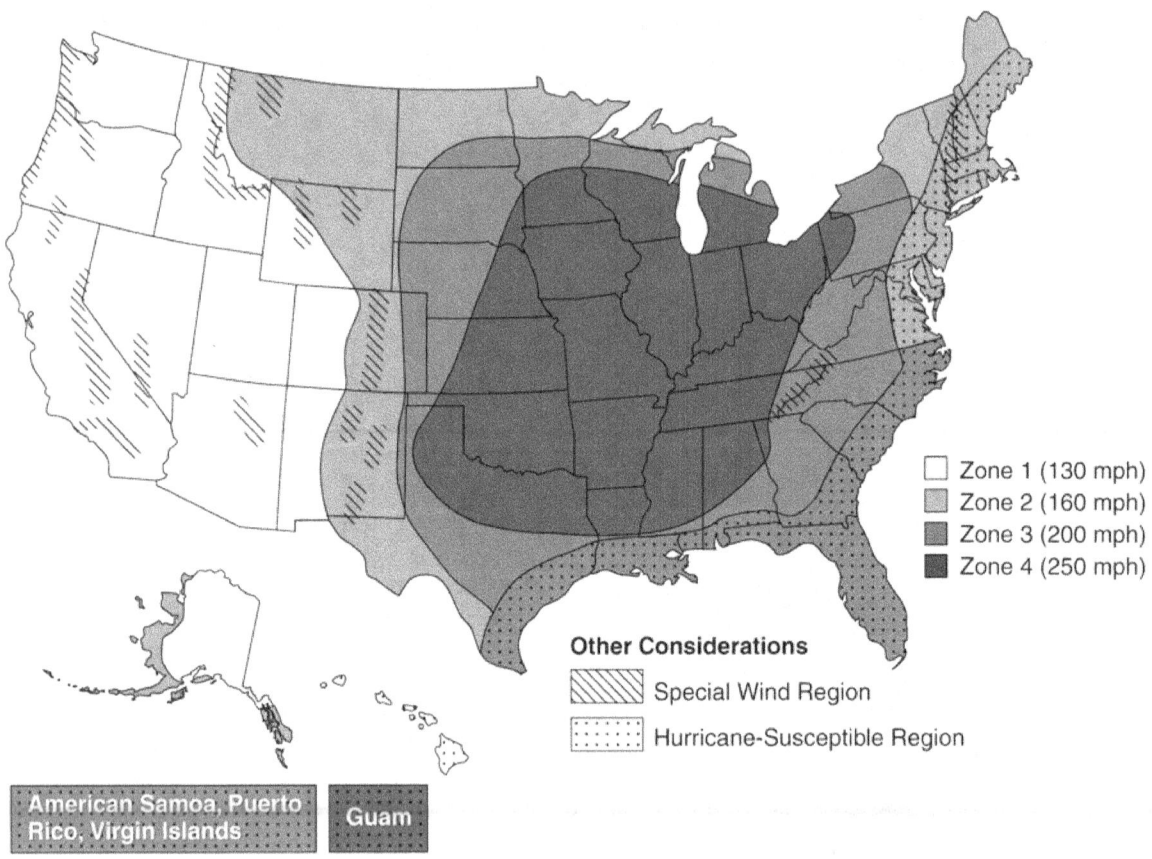

Figure 1. Map of the United States Showing Maximum Wind Velocities by Zone
The map key shows the wind velocity for Zone 1 at 130 mph, Zone 2 shows the wind velocity at 160 mph, Zone 3 shows the wind velocity at 200 mph, and Zone 4 shows the wind velocity at 250 mph. Other considerations shown include the special wind region and the hurricane susceptible region.

Lesson 3. Protecting Against Wind Damage

How Great Is Your Risk of Wind Damage?

Your home or place of business may be located near a coastal area that is subject to hurricane-force winds, or you may live in an area at risk for tornadoes.

The map on the preceding page titled "Wind Zones in the United States" shows areas that are susceptible to hurricanes and high winds.

Self-Assessment Questions:

- In which zone is your house or place of business located?

    __ Zone I   __ Zone II   __ Zone III   __ Zone IV

- How high is the windspeed you might face? _____ mph.

One- and two-story wood frame houses are especially vulnerable to wind damage, as are manufactured homes.

Nonstructural Protective Measures

To protect against wind damage without making any structural changes to a building, you can:

- Identify and remove trees and branches that could fall on the building walls or roof, or on power lines.
- Identify and repair loose or damaged building components such as siding, soffit and fascia, shingles and roofing, brickwork, and brick chimneys.

A hurricane brings torrential rain, and severe rainstorms may accompany a tornado. Buildings damaged by wind often suffer water damage as well. Water driven by hurricane-force wind can enter through usually rain-tight openings, and rain entering through a damaged roof can lay waste to the inside of a building.

Make sure that items such as important documents and irreplaceable personal objects such as photographs are stored in a safe location, preferably in watertight containers. Consider putting extra cash and important papers in a safe deposit box at your bank.

Nonstructural Protective Measures (Continued)

Hurricane warnings are issued about 24 hours before the hurricane is predicted to hit your area. If your area is under a hurricane warning:

- Move breakable items away from doors and windows.
- Board up doors and windows.
- Bring in outdoor furniture and other personal property kept outdoors.
- Secure manufactured home anchors.
- Secure outbuildings.
- Secure or move boats.
- Turn off propane tanks.

Structural Protective Measures

The roof, doors, and windows of your house or place of business are potentially vulnerable to wind damage. When houses are exposed to hurricane forces, roofs are most susceptible to damage, followed by walls and openings.

Roofs can be protected from wind damage by:

- Ensuring that plywood roof sheathing is properly installed.
- Bracing roof trusses.
- Installing hurricane straps.

You can strengthen **doors and windows** by:

- Installing reinforcing bolt kits at the top and bottom of doors.
- Reinforcing garage doors.
- Installing storm shutters over windows.

This lesson will explain how you can protect your home or business from winds.

Lesson 3. Protecting Against Wind Damage

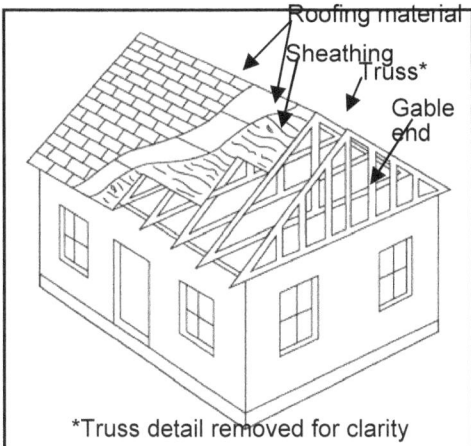

Figure 2

During a hurricane, wind forces are carried from the roof down to the exterior walls, down to the foundation. Homes can be damaged when wind forces are not properly transferred to the ground.

Figure 2 on the left shows the position of roof sheathing in the structure of a gabled roof. Roof sheathing (the boards or plywood nailed to the roof rafters or trusses) can fail during a hurricane if not properly installed. Examine the sheathing from the attic.

If many of the nails have missed the rafters, you may need to renail the sheathing.

If you are replacing your roof, make sure the sheathing complies with current recommended practices.

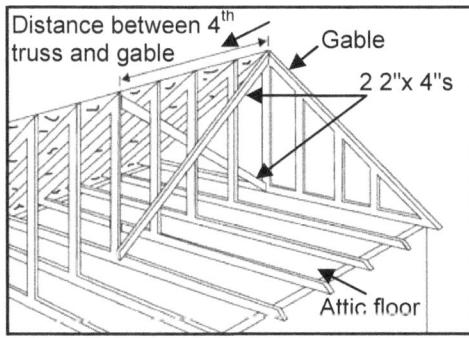

Figure 3

In a hurricane, the side walls of the roof (end gables) may take a real beating and collapse. Gable bracing often consists of 2"x 4"s placed in an "X" pattern at both ends of the attic: from the top center of the end gable to the bottom of the brace of the fourth truss, and from the bottom center of the end gable to the peak of the roof.

Figure 3 on the left shows gable bracing.

If your end gables do not appear to be braced, use a licensed contractor to install bracing. Ask your local building department whether a building permit is required for this work.

Protecting Roofs (Continued)

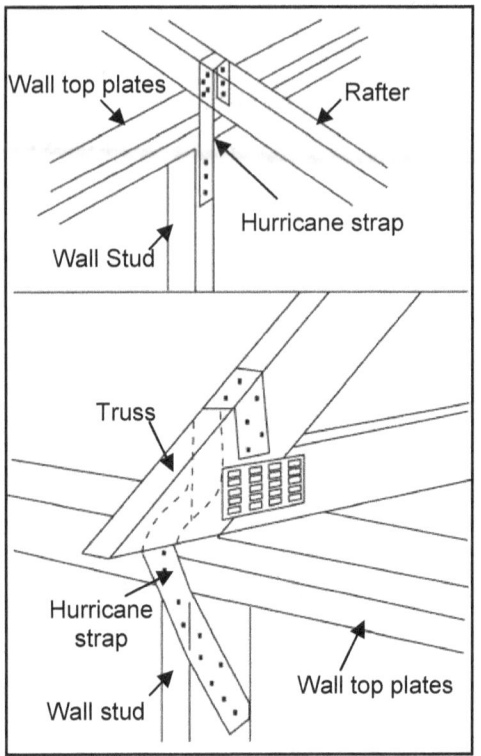

Figure 4
Top: Placement of Hurricane Straps on Rafters
Bottom: Placement of Hurricane Straps on Trusses

Hurricane straps (made out of galvanized metal) help keep the roof fastened to the walls in high winds. These straps are often difficult to install, so you may need a contractor for this project. Ask your building department whether hurricane straps are required or advisable in your area.

Protecting Doors

The exterior walls, doors, and windows are the protective shell of your home. If the shell is broken during a hurricane or tornado, high winds can enter the home and put pressure on the roof and walls, causing serious damage.

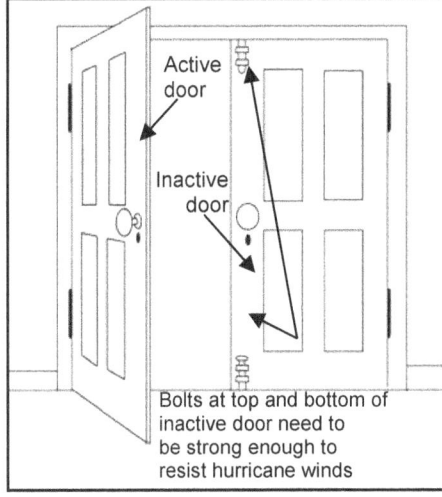

Active door

Inactive door

Bolts at top and bottom of inactive door need to be strong enough to resist hurricane winds

Figure 5. Reinforcement of Double Doors Within a Home

Double-Entry Doors

For each double door, at least one of the doors should be secured at both the top of the door frame and the floor with sturdy sliding bolts. Most bolts that come with double doors, however, are not strong enough to withstand high winds.

Your local hardware store can help you select the proper bolts. Some door manufacturers provide reinforcing bolt kits made specifically for their doors.

Protecting Doors: Garage Doors

If the garage door fails, winds can enter your home and blow out doors, windows, walls, and the roof.

Doublewide (two-car) garage doors can pose a problem during hurricanes because they are so large that they wobble as the high winds blow and can pull out of their tracks or collapse from wind pressure.

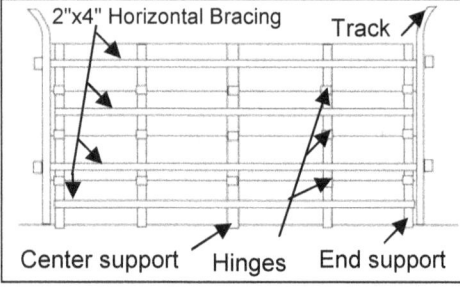

Figure 6. Reinforcement of Double Garage Doors

Some garage doors can be strengthened with retrofit kits. Many garage doors can be reinforced at their weakest points. Ask your building department for guidance on what to do.

Retrofitting your garage doors involves installing horizontal bracing onto each panel. This horizontal bracing may be available in a kit from the garage door manufacturer. You may also need heavier hinges and stronger center supports and end supports for your door.

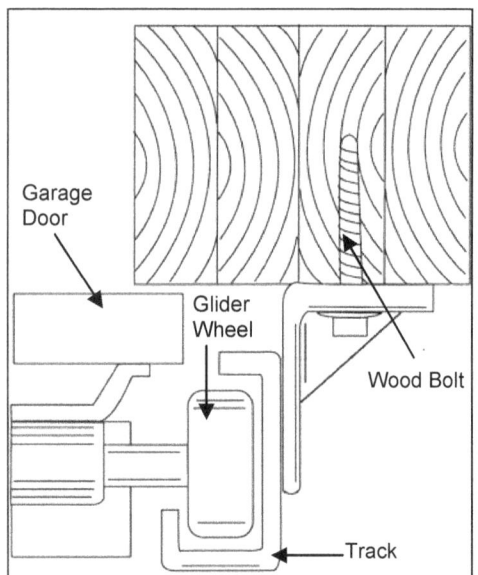

Figure 7. Garage Door Reinforcement

Check the track on your garage door. With both hands, grab a section of each track and see if it is loose or if it can be twisted. If so, a stronger track should be installed. Make sure that it is anchored to the 2"x 4"s inside the wall with heavy wood bolts or properly attached to masonry with expansion bolts.

Protecting Windows

Installing storm shutters is one of the best ways to protect your home or place of business from hurricane damage.

Purchase or make storm shutters for all exposed windows, glass surfaces, French doors, sliding glass doors, and skylights. There are many types of manufactured shutters made out of wood, steel, or aluminum. You can also make storm shutters with 5/8-inch thick exterior-grade plywood.

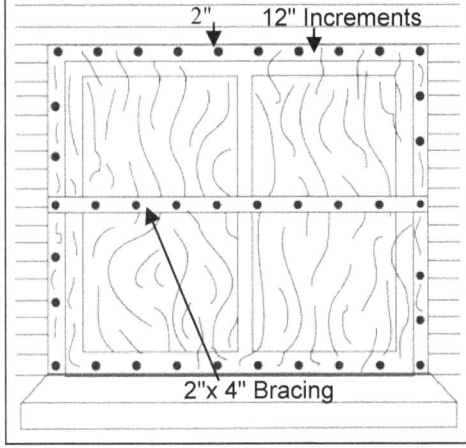

Plywood shutters that you make yourself, if installed properly, can offer a high level of protection from flying debris during a hurricane. Plywood shutters can be installed on all types of buildings.

Before installing shutters, check with your local building official to find out if a building permit is required.

It is important that you have your shutters ready now, and that you mark and store them so they can be easily installed during a hurricane watch.

Figure 8. Two Methods for Installing Plywood Shutters

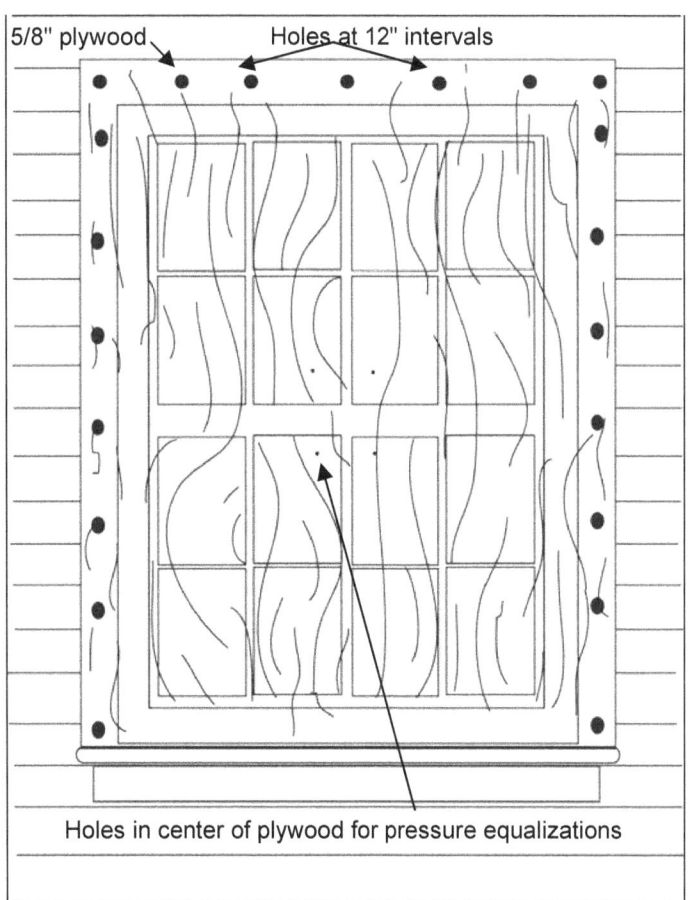

Tornado Risks

A tornado is a violent windstorm characterized by a twisting, funnel-shaped cloud. Tornadoes have been recorded in all 50 states, though they form most typically in a broad area of the American Midwest and South. The below map, "Tornado Risk Areas in the Continental United States," shows the relative risk of tornadoes.

Tornado Risk Areas in the Continental United States

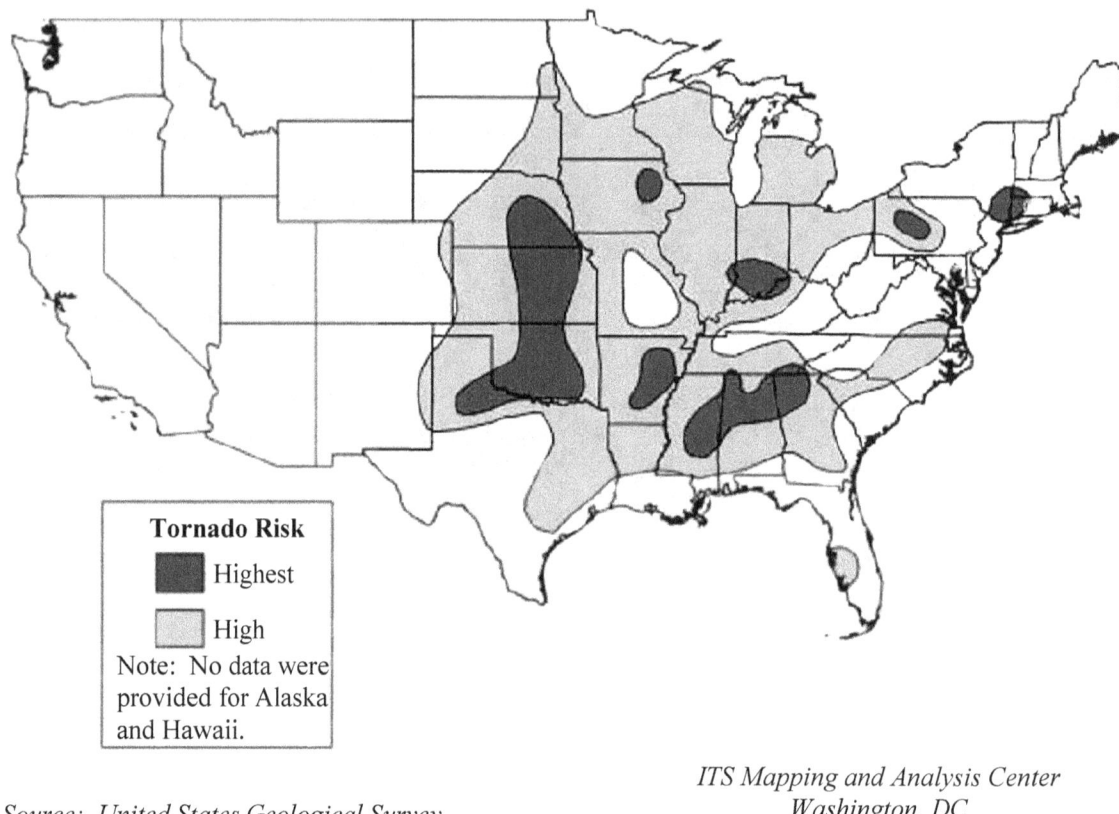

Tornado Risk
- ■ Highest
- ▨ High

Note: No data were provided for Alaska and Hawaii.

ITS Mapping and Analysis Center
Washington, DC

Source: United States Geological Survey

**Figure 9. Map of the United States Showing Areas
at Low, High, and Highest Risk of Tornadoes**

Highest Risk States: Portions of OK, AR, IA, IN, MS, AL, GA, PA, NY
High Risk States: Portions of NE, KS, OK, TX, AR, MS, AL, TN, GA, SC, NC, KY, IN, IL, MO, IA, WI, MI, PA, FL

Self-Assessment Question:

Is your house or place of business located in an area of:

☐ Highest Risk   ☐ High Risk   ☐ Low Risk

Tornado Risks: Safe Rooms

When severe weather threatens, individuals and families community-wide need advance warning and protection from the dangerous forces of extreme winds. You may want to consider a safe room to protect you and your family from the high winds.

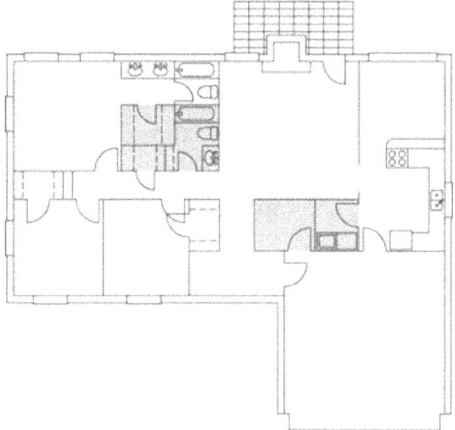

Figure 10. Possible Safe Room Locations

The purpose of a safe room or a wind shelter is to provide a space to seek refuge that provides a high level of protection. You can build a safe room in one of several places in your home or place of business:

- The basement.
- Atop a concrete slab-on-grade foundation or garage floor.
- An interior room on the first floor.

Safe rooms built below ground level provide the greatest protection, but a safe room built in a first-floor interior room also can provide the necessary protection. Below-ground safe rooms must be designed to avoid accumulating water during the heavy rains that often accompany severe windstorms.

To protect its occupants, a safe room must be built to withstand high winds and flying debris, even if the rest of the building is severely damaged or destroyed. Consider the following when building a safe room:

- The safe room must be adequately anchored to resist overturning and uplift.
- The walls, ceiling, and door of the shelter must withstand wind pressure and resist penetration by windborne objects and falling debris.

The connections between all parts of the safe room must be strong enough to resist the wind. Sections of either interior or exterior building walls that are used as walls of the safe room must be separated from the structure of the building so that damage to the building will not cause damage to the safe room.

Tornado Risks: Safe Rooms (Continued)

References

Specific guidance is available from FEMA on the construction of both residential safe rooms and community shelters.

- Taking Shelter From the Storm: Building a Safe Room Inside Your House. L-233.
  Brochure providing details about obtaining information on how to build a wind-safe room to withstand tornado, hurricane, and other high winds.

- Taking Shelter From the Storm: Building a Safe Room Inside Your House. FEMA-320.
  Manual with detailed information about how to build a wind-safe room to withstand tornado, hurricane, and other high winds.

Web link: http://www.fema.gov/mit/saferoom/

Protecting Your Place of Business

When a place of business is damaged, the business owner faces the cost to repair or replace the building(s). In addition, the business can suffer loss of inventory, business interruption, and loss of wages for employees.

Structural measures recommended to protect your place of business from wind damage are:

- Use threaded fasteners to attach metal roof decking. Welds are often unable to carry uplift loads.
- In tornado-prone areas, use enhanced wind design for roof coverings on essential buildings.
- Use adequate ties to foundations and roofs when reinforcing concrete and partially reinforced masonry.
- Make ties between concrete and other materials with drilled-in fasteners or cast-in-place fasteners.
- Engineer and construct masonry walls to support the specific architecture of the building (i.e., exterior wall panels, parapets, and decorative finishes). Diaphragm action to resist wind-generated shear forces must be maintained and reinforcement must be properly placed in concrete and masonry walls to reduce the possibility of collapse during high wind storms.
- Use anchors in precast concrete buildings to prevent the uplift of hollow core planks and other precast elements during high winds.
- Avoid the use of powder-driven anchors to attach bottom plates of walls to concrete unless the anchors are very closely spaced to resist pull-out.
- Minimize the creation of windborne debris by appropriately designing, manufacturing, and installing architectural features.

Lesson 3. Protecting Against Wind Damage

To read more about Success Stories, go to <u>New Success Story Site</u>.

Moore, Oklahoma

Don Staley and his family are no strangers to storms and tornadoes. Their first home was hit by a tornado in October 1998 and suffered minor damage but was destroyed by another tornado on May 3, 1999. They rode out both storms inside the house. "It was such a frightening sound," he said. "We decided we weren't going to ride out another one inside the house."

In December 2000, the Staley's new home was ready. Shortly after moving in, they had an above-ground safe room constructed on the back patio. The concrete room has 8-inch thick walls, an 18-inch thick ceiling, a 10-inch foundation, and a sliding entry door made of 12-gauge steel with three-quarter inch plywood on each side. The safe room is equipped with battery-powered lights and a battery-powered television.

When the warning sirens sounded on May 8, 2003, Don took shelter in the safe room along with his dog and two cats to ride out the storm feeling very protected and safe. "I was watching it on TV in there," he recalled. "I could see it was coming my way and I could hear it coming. I could hear the roar. That's a sound you never forget."

When he emerged from the shelter, he found his house in shambles with the roof ripped off. Other houses on the street were also heavily damaged or destroyed. The Staleys used their safe room following the tornado to store and protect belongings they had salvaged.

The Staley's home was among the more than 300 homes destroyed in the city that day. Whereas a severe tornado that hit the city in May of 1999 claimed 44 lives, there were no deaths in the 2003 tornado. The absence of fatalities is being attributed to community preparedness, improved early warning systems, and the many safe rooms and shelters that have been built.

Staley sums it all up, "The safe room saved my life, it came through with flying colors. It's worth a million bucks to me."

Lesson 3. Protecting Against Wind Damage

Charlotte Harbor, Florida

Hurricane Charley came to Charlotte Harbor one Friday, with winds up to 114 mph, leaving the community stunned. Buildings were destroyed, and streets were filled with debris and downed power lines. While the storm was swirling through town, 30 newspaper employees braved the storm at their office unable to get home. They were dry and secure because the structure was built to resist strong winds and the windows were fitted with storm shutters.

In the mid-1990s, Richard Hackney, Vice President of Operations, lobbied the stockholders for storm shutters to protect the *Sun* newspaper building in Charlotte Harbor. His experience with Hurricane Andrew taught him that an investment would be worth it. The shareholders agreed, and the shutters were purchased for $15,000.

When installed, storm shutters maintain building integrity by protecting the windows from direct wind pressure and windborne debris. If flying debris breached large office windows, wind-driven rain could enter and cause the loss of valuable computers containing information on news stories, research, subscribers, and other files. Intense winds coming in through these windows would cause "uplift" pressure on the roof system. Pressure inside the building, along with the speed of the wind above the roof surface, could lift the roof causing catastrophic damage to the building, its contents, and anyone working inside.

According to David Dunn-Rankin, President of the *Sun*, "The shutters helped keep the roof on and kept us operational. If we had lost the roof…I don't know…it's frightening. Lost revenue, subscriber credits, computer replacement, press equipment repairs or replacement, and production outsourcing all add up. We could have been looking at $3 million to get us back to where we could put out the paper here."

The entire Charlotte Harbor area was without power, but even that did not stop the *Sun* from publishing. The paper was without power for 14 days. However, because the building integrity had been maintained, they were otherwise operational. Instead of shutting down, they hooked up a rented, 1750KV generator, and published the newspaper.

"We didn't miss a beat," said Dunn-Rankin.

"It's not just about the dollars, it's about publishing." said Hackney. "It's not even an option not to publish. We have to be able to protect our people, our building, our presses, and maintain our capacity to publish. We met our goal."

The *Sun* came out on the Monday following Charley's hit on Friday.

Lesson 3. Protecting Against Wind Damage

This lesson reviewed the following steps you can take to protect your home or business against wind damage.

☐ Know your risk of wind damage. Certain areas have a high risk of damage from hurricanes, tornadoes, or high winds.

☐ Remove overhanging and dead tree limbs that could fall on buildings or power lines.

☐ Repair loose or damaged building components such as siding and roof shingles.

☐ Place important possessions and valuables in safe locations.

☐ Secure:

- Manufactured home anchors.
- Outbuildings.
- Boats.

☐ Move breakable items away from doors and windows. Board up doors and windows.

☐ Bring in outdoor furniture and other personal property kept outdoors.

☐ Turn off propane tanks.

☐ Make structural changes, including:

- Bracing and strapping the roof.
- Making doors and garage doors more wind-resistant.
- Installing storm shutters on windows.

☐ Consider building a safe room to protect against tornadoes.

☐ As you construct or modify your place of business, design for wind resistance by incorporating recommended fasteners, ties, reinforcements, and anchors.

The protective measures you consider depend on where your house or business is located.

Is your location vulnerable to hurricanes, or at high risk of tornadoes? If so, decide which protective measures make the most sense in your situation.

- Take appropriate nonstructural protective measures.
- Consider whether retrofitting and/or building a safe room would be advisable.

Lesson 3. Protecting Against Wind Damage

The questions below review key points in protecting against wind damage. After completing the questions, you can check your answers on the answer sheet located after the course glossary.

1. Hurricanes can be predicted, so you have 2 to 3 days to prepare, but

   _____ strike with little warning.

2. Mark any of the following structures that are especially susceptible to wind damage.

   ☐ Brick houses

   ☐ One- and two-story wood-frame houses

   ☐ Manufactured homes

   ☐ Steel-frame commercial buildings

3. Write below three protective, **nonstructural** measures you can take in the 24 hours before a hurricane is predicted to hit your area.

   _____

   _____

   _____

4. Select the protective measure on the right that would be used to protect the structure on the left, and write the appropriate letter on each blank space.

   __ Roof   a. Secure with sliding bolts

   __ Double-entry doors   b. Install horizontal bracing

   __ Garage door   c. Install hurricane straps

   __ Window   d. Buy or make storm shutters

5. Safe rooms built below ground level provide the greatest protection.

   _____ True   _____ False

Introduction

Wildfires may begin in the wildland/urban interface or in remote spots where nobody notices them and then spread quickly, igniting brush, trees, and buildings.

An increasing number of people are choosing to live in woodland settings, in or near forests, rural areas, or remote mountain sites. These homeowners enjoy the beauty that comes from being close to nature, but also face the danger of wildfire.

Wildfires are most frequent in the West, but all wooded, brush, and grassy areas are vulnerable. Kansas, Mississippi, Louisiana, Georgia, Florida, the Carolinas, Tennessee, California, and Massachusetts are especially prone to wildfires.

Classes of wildland fires include:

- Surface fires and ground fires, which burn along the ground. Surface fires are most common, and generally are started by people. Ground fires may burn on or below the ground, and usually are started by lightning.
- Crown fires that spread rapidly by wind, and move quickly by jumping along the tops of trees.

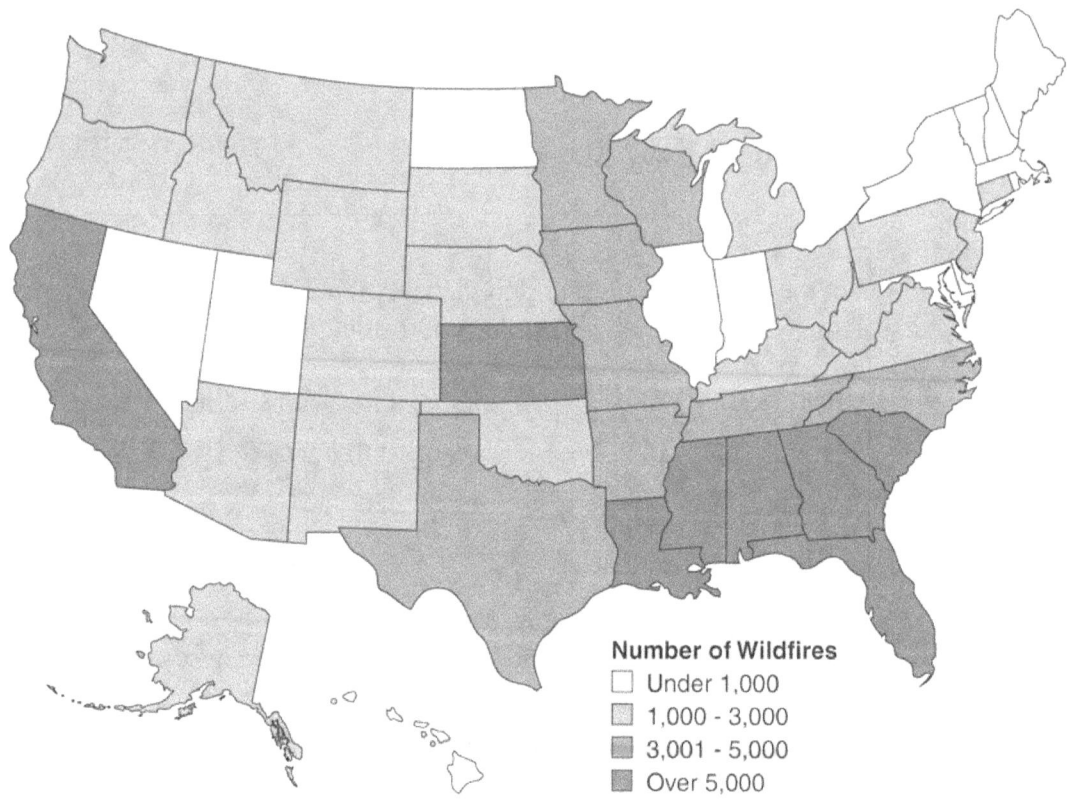

Figure 1. Typical Annual Wildfire Frequency by State

How Great Is Your Risk of Wildfire?

If you live or own a business in a wooded or rural setting, your home and/or place of business may be susceptible to wildfires.

The map on the preceding page shows typical frequency for wildfires among States in the United States.

Self-Assessment Questions:

- How many wildfires occur in your State in a typical year?

  __ Under 1,000   __ 1,000-3,000   __ 3,000-5,000   __ Over 5,000

- Is your home or business located in or near a wooded or wildland area?

  __ Yes   __ No

Contact your local fire marshal, local forestry representative, building official, city engineer, or planning and zoning administrator to find our whether your home or place of business is in a wildfire hazard area.

Nonstructural Protective Measures

You can make your home or place of business more resistant to fire damage by taking the steps below.

- Regularly clean roof and gutters.
- Inspect chimneys at least twice a year. Clean them at least once a year. Keep the dampers in good working order. Equip chimneys and stovepipes with a spark arrester that meets the requirements of National Fire Protection Association Code 211. (Contact your local fire department for exact specifications on building codes.)
- Use 1/2-inch mesh screen beneath porches, decks, floor areas, and the home itself. Also, screen openings to floors, roof, and attic.
- Consider installing protective shutters or heavy fire-resistant drapes.
- Plant fire-resistant shrubs and trees. For example, hardwood trees are less flammable than pine, evergreen, eucalyptus, or fir trees. Introduce more native vegetation.

Creating a Safety Zone

You can create a 30- to 100-foot safety zone around your home or place of business. Within this zone, you can take steps to reduce potential exposure to flames and radiant heat.

Buildings in pine forests should have a minimum safety zone of 100 feet. If the structure sits on a steep slope, standard protective measures may not suffice. Contact your local fire department or forestry office for additional information.

To create a safety zone, take the following steps:

- Remove leaves and rubbish from under structures.
- Thin a 15-foot space between tree crowns, and remove limbs within 15 feet of the ground.
- Remove dead branches that extend over the roof.
- Prune tree branches and shrubs within 15 feet of a stovepipe or chimney outlet.
- Ask the power company to clear branches from power lines.
- Remove vines from the walls of the home.
- Mow grass regularly.
- Do not connect wooden fencing directly to your home.
- Clear a 10-foot area around propane tanks and the barbecue. Place a screen over the grill, using nonflammable material with mesh no coarser than one-quarter inch.
- Regularly dispose of newspapers and rubbish at an approved site. Follow local burning regulations.
- Place stove, fireplace, and grill ashes in a metal bucket, soak in water for 2 days, then bury the cold ashes in mineral soil.
- Store gasoline, oily rags, and other flammable materials in approved safety cans. Place cans in a safe location away from the base of buildings.
- Stack firewood at least 100 feet away and uphill from the building. Clear combustible material within 20 feet. Use only UL-approved woodburning devices.

As shown in the figure, you should clear the area around your house. Rake leaves, dead limbs, and twigs. Clear all flammable vegetation.

The distance between your house and any nearby tree should always be greater than the height of the mature tree or at least 10 feet. Similarly, any outbuildings, such as storage sheds, should be at least as far away as their height.

Figure 2. Clearance Around a Building

Planning Water Needs

If a wildfire threatens your home or place of business, you will need access to water to douse flames and wet the roof or other building and landscape components to prevent ignition. Think ahead to identify a water source and ways to deliver water to fire sites.

- Identify and maintain an adequate outside water source such as a small pond, cistern, well, swimming pool, or hydrant.
- Have a garden hose(s) that is long enough to reach any area of the home and other structures on the property.
- Install freeze-proof exterior water outlets on at least two sides of the home and near other structures on the property. Install additional outlets at least 50 feet from the home.
- Consider obtaining a portable gasoline-powered pump in case electrical power is cut off.

Structural Protective Measures

Design and landscape your home with wildfire safety in mind. Select materials and plants that can help contain fire rather than fuel it.

- Use fire-resistant or noncombustible materials on the roof and exterior structure of the dwelling, or treat wood or combustible material used in roofs, siding, decking, or trim with UL-approved fire-retardant chemicals.
- Box in the eaves, fascias, soffits, and subfloors with fire-resistant materials like treated wood, reducing the vent sizes.
- Enclose the underside of decks with fire-resistant materials.
- Cover exterior walls with fire-resistant materials like stucco, stone, or brick. (Vinyl siding can melt and is not recommended.)
- Use double-paned or tempered glass for all exterior windows.

Some roofing materials, including asphalt shingles and especially wood shakes, are less resistant to fire than others. When wildfires and brush fires spread to houses, it is often because burning branches, leaves, and other debris buoyed by the heated air and carried by the wind fall on roofs. If the roof of your house is covered with wood or asphalt shingles, you should consider replacing them with fire-resistant materials.

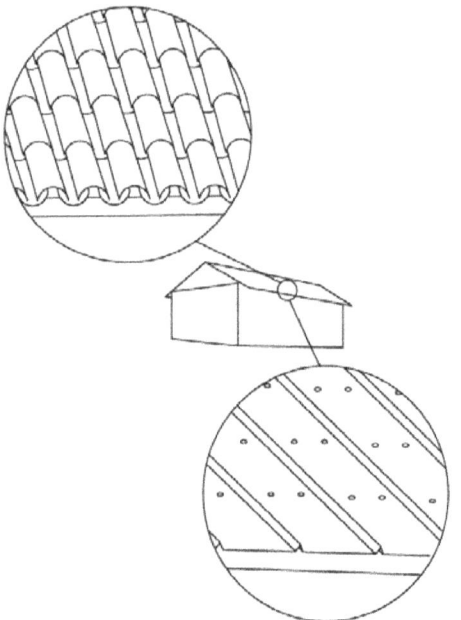

As shown in the figure, you can replace your existing roofing materials with slate, terra cotta or other types of tile, or standing-seam metal roofing.

Replacing roofing materials is difficult and dangerous work. Unless you are skilled in roofing and have all the necessary tools and equipment, you will probably want to hire a roofing contractor to do the work. Also a roofing contractor can advise you on the relative advantages and disadvantages of various fire-resistant roofing materials.

Figure 3. Fire-Resistant Roofing

Personal Safety Measures

You can take a number of steps to promote the personal safety of your family, neighbors, and/or employees.

- Make sure that fire vehicles can get to your home or place of business. Clearly mark all driveway entrances and display your name and address. Install noncombustible street signs.
- Post fire emergency telephone numbers.
- Plan several escape routes away from your home or business site—by car and by foot.
- Talk to your neighbors about wildfire safety. Plan how the neighborhood could work together if a wildfire threatens.
- Consider how you could help neighbors who have special needs such as elderly or disabled persons. Make plans to take care of children who may be on their own if parents can't get home.
- Install a smoke alarm on each level of your home, especially near and in bedrooms; test monthly and change the batteries two times each year. (For commercial buildings, local building codes usually specify requirements for smoke detectors and automatic sprinkler systems.)
- Teach each family member or employee how to use the fire extinguisher (ABC type) and show them where it's kept.
- Keep an approved ladder that will reach the roof of the building. Do not use if not comfortable on the ladder.
- Keep handy household items that can be used as fire tools: a rake, axe, handsaw or chainsaw, bucket, and shovel.
- Only fight fire if you are comfortable to do so. Ask for training from your local fire department.

Before You Evacuate

If you are warned that a wildfire is threatening your area, listen to your radio for reports and evacuation information. Have a battery-operated radio available. Follow the instructions of local officials.

If you're sure you have time, take steps to protect your home or place of business before evacuating.

Inside

- Close windows, vents, doors, venetian blinds, noncombustible window coverings, and heavy drapes. Remove lightweight curtains.
- Shut off gas at the meter. Turn off pilot lights.
- Open fireplace damper. Close fireplace screens. Move flammable furniture into the center of the home away from windows and sliding-glass doors.
- Turn on a light in each room to increase the visibility of your home or place of business in heavy smoke.
- Gather pets into one room. Make plans to care for your pets when you evacuate.
- Arrange temporary housing at a friend or relative's home or a hotel outside the threatened area.

Outside

- Back your car into the garage or park it in an open space facing the direction of escape. Shut doors and roll up windows. Leave the key in the ignition. Ensure car does not lock when exiting the car.
- Close garage windows and doors, but leave them unlocked. Disconnect automatic garage door openers.
- Seal attic and ground vents with pre-cut plywood or commercial seals.
- Turn off propane tanks.
- Place combustible patio furniture inside.
- Connect the garden hose to outside taps.
- Set up the portable gasoline-powered water pump.
- Place lawn sprinklers on the roof and near aboveground fuel tanks. Wet the roof.
- Wet or remove shrubs within 15 feet of the home.
- Gather fire tools.

Success Stories

Los Angeles County, California

For Karen Stevens, her family, and neighbors in the Southern Oaks section of Stevenson Ranch, it was a blessing that the planned development where they live has a 200-foot-wide greenbelt around it designed to ward off wildfires. "There were plenty of embers flying around," said Stevens, whose home in Santa Clarita backs up to the Santa Susana Mountains.

These same mountains were set ablaze by the Simi Fire, one of 12 wildfires that burned more than 739,000 acres in five Southern California counties in October 2003. Airdrops were made on the wildfire as it came toward the Stevens' home, and firefighters surrounded the area. Firefighters were bolstered in their fight by the mitigation measures taken.

Homes in the Stevenson Ranch planned development were all built to conform to Los Angeles County building and fire codes. All developers must comply with codes before building permits are issued. There is a multi-hazard approach to disaster-resistant construction. Wildfire mitigation measures include double-pane heat-resistant windows, concrete-slate tile roofing materials, and enclosed eaves as primary protective measures standard. There are 100-foot greenbelts planted with fire-resistant plant materials, and they have sprinkler systems. The maintenance of greenbelts is managed through the homeowners association.

To mitigate against earthquakes, homes are built on high-tension slabs and bolted onto the slabs. "Earthquake safety was important to us when we were considering buying a home here," said Todd Stevens. "Since the experience of the wildfires, we're very grateful for the wildfire protective measures that are required." Clearly, pre-fire mitigation, which cost less money than the value of the home, has protected this family's investment.

Note: This success story shows that the couple was more focused on the earthquake hazard when they bought the house, and didn't fully appreciate the fire provisions until after they were tested by a fire.

Success Stories (Continued)

Los Alamos, New Mexico

When John and Cindia Hogan bought their home in 1994, they did so knowing that a major fire might occur in the Santa Fe National Forest that backs up to their property. John Hogan, a physical scientist with the U.S. Geological Survey and a trained, experienced firefighter, began taking steps to mitigate their home in 1996.

In 1996, Hogan contracted to have a metal roof put on their two-story, wood-frame, 2,600-square foot home located on two-thirds of an acre. He also cleared some 100 trees from the rear portion of the property, and removed flammable materials from the backyard. The cost of mitigation is estimated at about $50,000. All costs were borne by the Hogan family.

On May 10, 2000, the Hogan family evacuated from their home, and on May 11 the Cerro Grande fire—largest wildfire in New Mexico history to date—burned through their neighborhood and other areas of the community of Los Alamos. For 2 days, the Hogans believed their home was consumed by the blaze, which burned and destroyed well over 200 homes, leaving more than 400 families and individuals homeless.

But when John and Cindia Hogan returned to their home, they found it and one other adjacent house intact. Homes to the west and south of them had been destroyed. "We're very conscious of fire danger," Hogan said. "We consciously chose fire mitigation as a proper move." Hogan plans on more mitigation, including removal of more trees in his yard, and put fire retardant on cedar shake paneling on the east and west walls of his home.

The most valuable information that Hogan had was his knowledge of landscape ecology, based on his work with the U.S. Geological Survey. He works with vegetation studies and fire history as well as changes in landscape.

The Cerro Grande fire caused one tree in the Hogans' front yard to catch fire, and burned a shed and its contents at the far rear of their backyard. The only other damage from the fire was soot that entered into the dryer vent.

The home is insured for $270,000 for its structure and another $200,000 for contents. The savings, even though his property is insured, are figured at more than $450,000—the value of the structure and its contents—nine times the cost of mitigating the structure and grounds.

Of the expense of mitigating his home, Hogan said, "It was certainly worth it."

Lesson 4. Protecting Against Wildfires

This lesson reviewed the following steps you can take to protect your home or business against wildfires.

- ☐ Regularly clean the roof, gutters, and chimney.
- ☐ Put mesh screening over openings.
- ☐ Consider installing protective shutters or heavy fire-resistant drapes.
- ☐ Box in the eaves, fascias, soffits, and subfloors with fire-resistant materials like treated wood, reducing the vent sizes.
- ☐ Enclose the underside of decks with fire-resistant materials.
- ☐ Cover exterior walls with fire-resistant materials like stucco, stone, or brick. (Vinyl siding can melt and is not recommended.)
- ☐ Use double-paned or tempered glass for all exterior windows.
- ☐ Create a 30- to 100-foot safety zone by removing or trimming trees and eliminating or reducing flammable materials in the area around your home or place of business.
- ☐ Ensure there is a water supply that can be used to fight fire on your property, if you are comfortable to do so.
- ☐ Select plants that can help contain fire rather than fuel it.
- ☐ Replace existing roofing materials with fire-resistant roofing.

Wildfire Protection Resources

A number of resources offer indepth information that can help you learn more about particular wildfire protection options.

To obtain copies of the documents listed below and other FEMA documents, call FEMA Publications at 1-800-480-2520. Information is also available on the FEMA website at http://www.fema.gov.

- Protecting Your Property From Fire: Dealing With Vegetation and Combustible Materials, http://www.fema.gov/fima/how2001.shtm
- Protecting Your Property From Fire: Roofing, http://www.fema.gov/fima/how2002.shtm
- "Five Hot Tips for Homeowners on the Edge," by Herbert McLean, in *American Forest*, vol. 99, no. 5-6, 1993
- *Guide to Landscaping for Fire Safety,* 2nd. Ed., University of California, 1992
- "Firescaping: Ways To Keep Your House and Garden from Going up in Smoke," by Joan Boulton in *Horticulture, The Magazine of American Gardening*, vol. 69, no. 8, 1991
- Protecting Residences From Wildfires: A Guide for Homeowners, Lawmakers, and Planners, Technical Report No. 50, U.S. Department of Agriculture, 1981
- Information is also available from the National Roofing Contractors Association, 1-800-323-9545.

Other websites offer information on protecting against wildfires, including:

- Institute for Business and Home Safety, http://www.IBHS.org
- National Fire Protection Association, http://www.nfpa.org
- Firewise Communities, http://www.firewise.org/communities

Lesson 4. Protecting Against Wildfires

The questions below review key points in protecting against wildfires. After completing the questions, you can check your answers on the answer sheet located after the course glossary.

1. The most common type of wildfire is a surface fire, which generally is started by _____.

2. Fire-resistant roofing materials include: (Mark all that apply.)

    ☐   Tile roofing

    ☐   Asphalt shingles

    ☐   Metal roofing

    ☐   Wood shakes

3. Identify three measures that can be used to create a safety zone around a home or place of business.

    _____

    _____

    _____

4. Select the measure on the right that would be used to protect the item on the left, and write the appropriate letter on each blank space.

    ___ Openings   a.   Cover with mesh screening

    ___ Chimneys   b.   Clean regularly

    ___ Gutters

    ___ Barbeque grill

5. States located east of the Mississippi River do not experience wildfires.

    ___ True   ___ False

Introduction

After an earthquake hits, it's too late to protect your home or business from damage. But you can limit future earthquake damage. Sometimes, a little time and a few dollars are all you need.

How Great Is Your Risk of Earthquake Damage?

About 5,000 earthquakes can be felt each year in the United States. Earthquakes occur most frequently west of the Rocky Mountains. Historically, however, the most violent earthquakes struck the central United States. All 50 States and all U.S. territories are vulnerable to earthquakes. Forty-one States or territories are at moderate to high risk. Since 1900, earthquakes have hit 39 States.

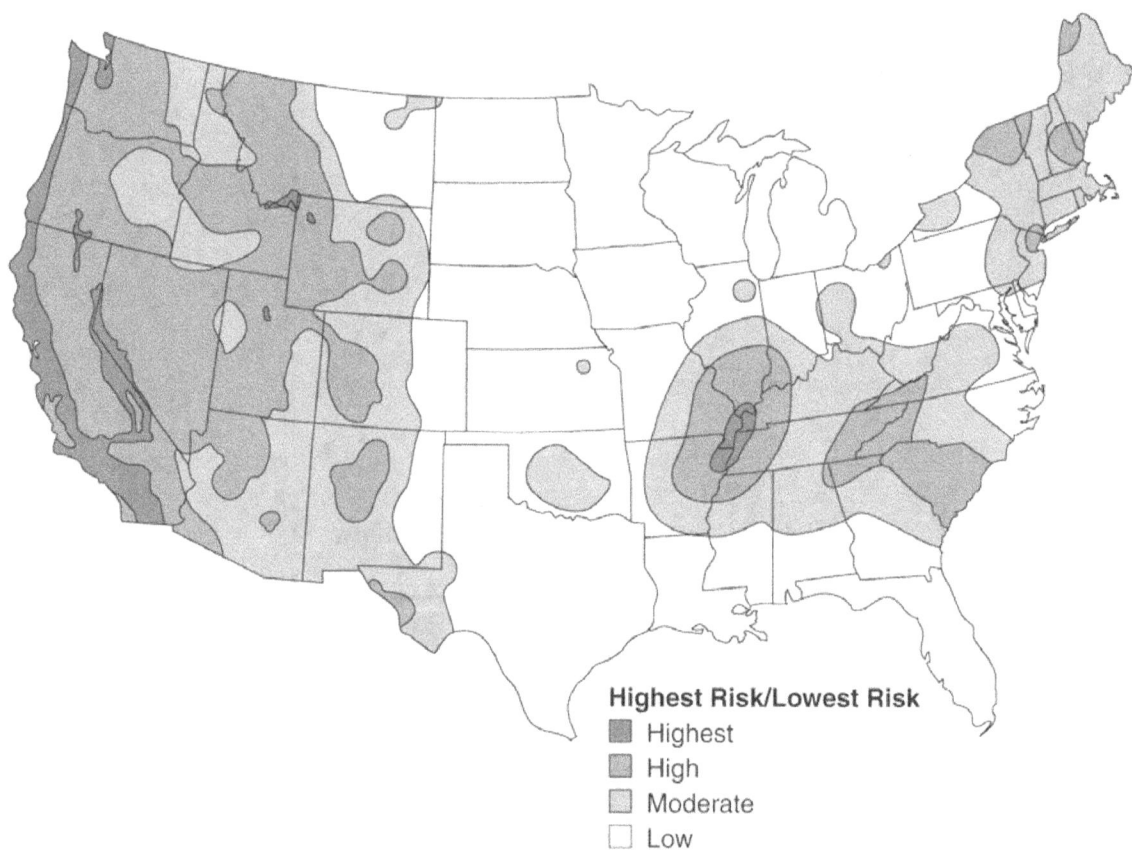

Highest Risk/Lowest Risk
- Highest
- High
- Moderate
- Low

Figure 1. Seismic Hazard Map

How Great Is Your Risk of Earthquake Damage? (Continued)

Self-Assessment Questions:

- Is your home and/or business located west of the Rocky Mountains?

  __ Yes   __ No

- Is your home and/or business located in one of the following areas?

  - Northeastern Arkansas
  - Southeastern Missouri
  - Western Tennessee
  - Kentucky
  - Southern Illinois

    __ Yes   __ No

- In which risk zone is your home or business located?

  __ Highest   __ High   __ Moderate   __ Low

Nonstructural Protective Measures

A number of measures can help to avoid earthquake damage, including:

- Securing heavy furniture and other items.
- Securing loose items and equipment.
- Fastening water heaters.
- Securing propane and fuel tanks.

Securing Heavy Items

Consider each piece of heavy, tall furniture in the building, such as bookcases, china hutches, and storage racks. Move or secure items that could fall over or block an exit in an earthquake.

Move heavy items, such as pictures, mirrors, or tall dressers, away from beds and places where people sit.

Securely anchor all large kitchen and laundry equipment to the floor, wall, or countertop, depending on the item. Such equipment includes:

- Stoves and ovens.
- Built-in and countertop microwave ovens.
- Garbage compactors.
- Dishwashers.
- Refrigerators and freezers.
- Clothes washers and dryers.
- Ironing equipment.

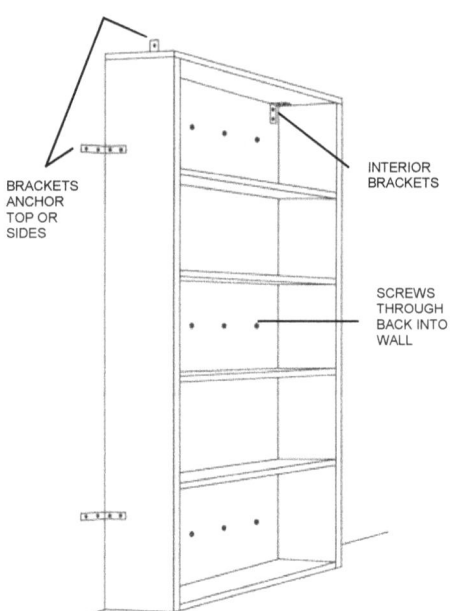

BRACKETS ANCHOR TOP OR SIDES

INTERIOR BRACKETS

SCREWS THROUGH BACK INTO WALL

Figure 2 shows methods to anchor heavy, tall furniture to vertical wall studs, concrete, or masonry with steel angle brackets.

Fasten heavy objects to the building structure and not just to a movable wall in your home or office.

Even large, heavy objects that appear stable should be secured to the wall. The heavier the furniture, the stronger the restraints need to be. A heavily loaded file cabinet requires much stronger restraints to keep it from overturning than a light file cabinet with the same dimensions.

Figure 2. Anchoring a Tall Bookcase

Securing Heavy Items (Continued)

Keep in mind some important guidelines for anchoring heavy items to walls or ceilings.

- Make sure the screws penetrate the studs behind the wall. Gypsum board, drywall, plaster, and other wall coverings are not strong enough to hold heavy furniture during an earthquake.
- For wood studs (typically located 16 or 24 inches on centers), use a minimum 1/4" diameter by 3" lag screws.
- For metal studs, use #12 sheet-metal screws long enough to penetrate the flange material. For concrete or masonry walls, use concrete anchor bolts.
- If wall studs do not line up with the furniture, consider installing a wood 2" x 4" or steel horizontal mounting strip to the studs near the top of the items to be anchored. Furniture can then be anchored to the mounting strip without regard to the stud locations.
- When possible, bolt file cabinets together (and to the wall studs) to form a more stable shape.
- Anchor eyebolts to wall studs for hanging heavy items such as pictures, mirrors, and shelving. Securely attach picture wires to picture frames.
- Make sure overhead light fixtures and hanging plants are anchored to the structural support above the ceiling. Ask a carpenter or an electrician to determine whether light fixtures and modular ceiling systems are securely fastened.

Securing Loose Items and Equipment

You can use a variety of methods and products to secure items stored in cabinets or placed on tables, desks, shelves, and countertops. Examples of products include adhesive-backed latches; nylon and elastic cords; wire, plastic, and elastic guardrails; and shelf edges to prevent equipment from falling on the floor.

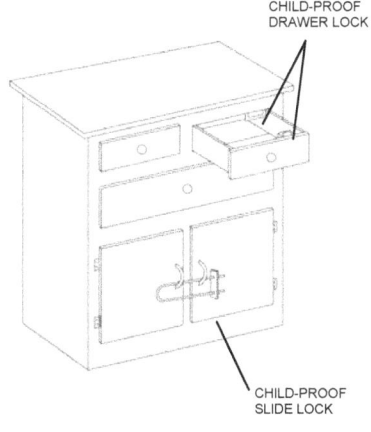

CHILD-PROOF
DRAWER LOCK

CHILD-PROOF
SLIDE LOCK

Figure 3. Securing Drawers and Cabinets

One way to prevent the accidental opening of drawers and cabinet doors is to install latches such as barrel bolts, safety hasps, and child-proof locks. Most hardware and home supply stores stock a variety of latches. Figure 3 shows two types of child-proof locks: one for drawers and one for cabinet doors. Most types of permanent latches can be installed easily and will not interfere with opening and closing of drawers and doors. The slide lock shown on the cabinet doors can be used on cabinets that do not need to be opened frequently; it is easily installed and removed.

Lesson 5. Protecting Against Earthquake Damage

To prevent damage to items stored in drawers and cabinets, you can:

- Put latches on cabinet doors, especially at home in your kitchen and at work or in school laboratories.
- Store breakable items such as bottled foods, glass, and china in low, closed cabinets with latches.
- Store weed killers, pesticides, and flammable products on bottom shelves in sturdy, closed, latched cabinets that are fastened to the wall or floor.

Following are some measures you can use to secure items on desks, tables, shelves, and countertops:

- Add lips to shelves to prevent costly items from sliding off their supports. Install edge restraints (such as wood molding) on bookshelves and storage shelves, or use elastic cords or wire guardrails to keep items from falling off open shelves.
- Fasten heavy or precious items to shelves or tables.
- Use easy tack putty to secure fragile objects on shelves.
- Keep breakable items in original packing boxes, when possible.
- Move incompatible chemicals to prevent mixing if the containers break.

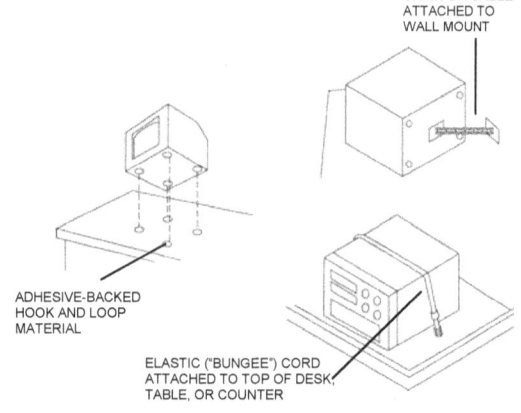

CHAIN OR CABLE ATTACHED TO WALL MOUNT

ADHESIVE-BACKED HOOK AND LOOP MATERIAL

ELASTIC ("BUNGEE") CORD ATTACHED TO TOP OF DESK, TABLE, OR COUNTER

Figure 4. Securing Computer Equipment

The tremors caused by even minor earthquakes can easily move personal computer systems, stereo systems, television sets, and other small appliances that typically sit on desks, tables, and countertops. If they fall, they can be damaged beyond repair.

As shown in Figure 4, you can protect desktop computers and other small appliances by restraining them in a variety of ways. Some methods, such as using hook-and-loop material (Velcro for example), require no tools. Others, which include using chain, cables, or elastic cord ("bungee" cords, for example), will usually require simple hand tools.

Fastening Water Heaters

Strapping the water heater to wall studs and having flexible gas and water lines installed will greatly reduce the risk of fire and water damage in an earthquake. All gas heaters and appliances should be connected to the gas pipe through flexible tubing.

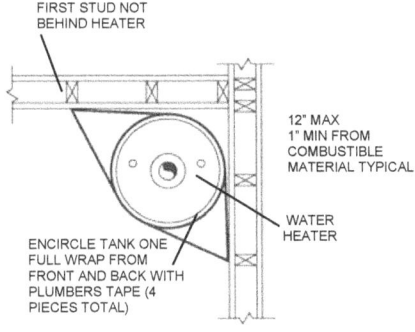

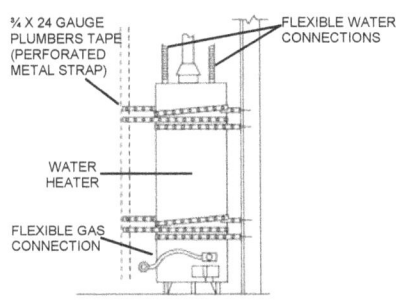

Figure 5 Top: Overhead View of a Water Heater Secured in a Corner or Closet: Bottom: Side View of a Water Heater Secured in a Corner or Closet

Figure 5 shows overhead and side views of a water heater secured in a corner or closet.

To secure a water heater in a corner or closet, you will need the following materials:

- 3/4" x 24-gauge perforated steel plumbers tape.
- 1/4" diameter x 3" lag screws and flat washers or 1/4" expandable anchors with 2" embedment for concrete or masonry walls.

Follow the directions below to secure a water heater in a corner or closet:

- The water heater should be 1" to 12" away from the corner walls.
- Locate the wall studs on both sides of the water heater (not behind it).
- Anchor plumbers tape (a flexible steel strap) to a wall stud with 1/4" diameter x 3" lag screw and flat washer.
- From about 9" from the top of the tank, wrap the plumbers tape all the way around the tank in a clockwise direction. Then anchor the tape to the stud on the other wall. Make sure the tape is tight.
- Repeat the process, again about 9" from the top of the tank, but this time wrap the tape in a counterclockwise direction.

Repeat the process two more times about 4" from the bottom of the tank. Wrap one band of tape in a clockwise direction and the other band of tape in a counterclockwise direction.

Fastening Water Heaters (Continued)

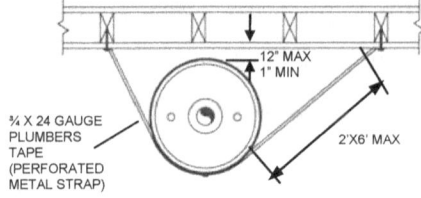

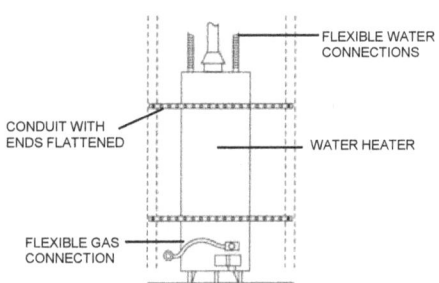

Figure 6
Top: Overhead View of a Water Heater Secured on a Straight Wall
Bottom: Side View of a Water Heater Secured on a Straight Wall

Figure 6 shows overhead and side views of a water heater secured on a straight wall.

To secure a water heater on a straight wall, you will need the following materials:

- 3/4" x 24-gauge perforated steel plumbers tape.
- 1/2" diameter conduit.
- 1/4" diameter x 1" round head machine screws with nuts and flat washers.
- 1/4" diameter x 3" lag screws and flat washer or 1/4" expandable anchors with 2" embedment for concrete or masonry walls.

Follow the directions below to secure a water heater on a straight wall:

- The water heater should be 1" to 12" away from the wall.
- Locate the wall studs on both sides of the water heater (not behind it).
- Wrap plumbers tape around the tank 9" from the top and 4" from the bottom. Secure tape with round head machine screw, flat washers, and nut.
- Cut four pieces of conduit to size. The conduit is used as angle bracing from the wall studs to the tank.
- Flatten 1" at each end of the conduit and bend 45 degrees. Drill holes 1/2" from each end.
- Anchor the conduit to the wall studs. Use 1/4" diameter x 3" lag screw and flat washer. Then anchor the conduit to the plumber's tape. Use 1/4" diameter x 1" round head machine screw, washer, and nut.

If you're using gas, have your utility company or a licensed plumber install a flexible hose where the gas line connects to the water heater at its base. Install flexible hoses for the water connections as well.

Lesson 5. Protecting Against Earthquake Damage

Anchoring Fuel Tanks and Wood-Burning Stoves

Fuel oil and propane tanks can slide or overturn in an earthquake, rupturing the tank or breaking the supply line and causing a fire. Even when a tank remains on its legs, the supply line can be ruptured. Escaping gas can then cause a fire.

Similar problems can occur with smaller, compressed gas cylinders, which are often stored inside a house or garage. Compressed gas cylinders have to be periodically replaced, and therefore cannot be permanently anchored, but you can use chains to attach them to a wall so that they will remain upright.

Take the following steps to secure fuel and propane tanks:

- Move tall, heavy objects that could fall and rupture the fuel or propane tank in an earthquake.
- Have a contractor install a flexible hose connection between the tank and supply line, and where the supply line enters the house.

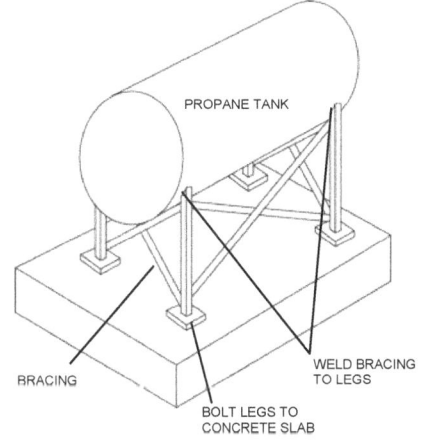

One way to prevent damage to propane tanks and compressed gas cylinders is to anchor and brace them securely.

Figure 7 shows how the legs of a propane tank can be braced and anchored.

Using a flexible connection on the supply line will help reduce the likelihood of a leak.

Figure 7. Securing a Propane Tank

Wood-burning and other free-standing stoves also pose a fire hazard in an earthquake. To secure a stove:

- Anchor the stove to the floor.
- Fasten stovepipe sections together to prevent separation.

You will most likely need a contractor for this work. Make sure all work conforms with local building codes.

Structural Protective Measures

You can make many changes yourself at relatively low cost if you have basic carpentry skills. Otherwise, contact a licensed professional about making the necessary changes to your home or business. Contact your local building department to modify details to fit local building codes.

If your home has a perimeter foundation, make sure the sill plate of the house is securely bolted to the foundation. Consult with your building department before deciding what to do.

A variety of products called "hold downs" are available for securing walls to the foundation.

Test the wood near the foundation by probing it with a pointed instrument. If you can penetrate the wood easily, it probably has wood decay and should be replaced with new pressure-treated wood.

Have a contractor inspect any deep cracks in the foundation.

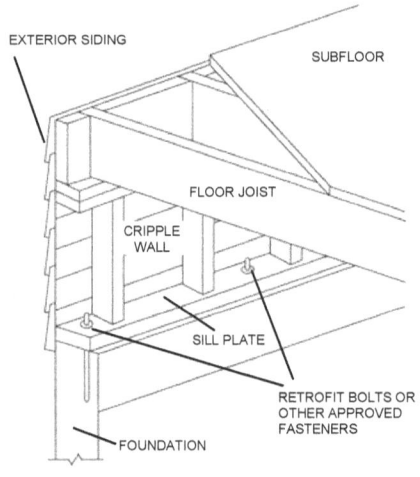

Figure 8. Sill Plate Bolted to Foundation

As shown in Figure 8, the sill plate of a house rests directly on top of the foundation. (This figure shows the sill plate for a house built on a cripple wall and crawl space foundation, a type of construction that is especially susceptible to earthquake damage.)

If the sill plate is not securely anchored, an earthquake can cause it to shift on the foundation. When this occurs, there is a greater potential for severe damage as well as injury to you and members of your family.

One way to increase the stability of your house and reduce earthquake damage is to have the sill plate bolted or otherwise anchored to the foundation. In the method shown in the figure, bolts long enough to pass through the sill plate and penetrate several inches into the foundation are installed every few feet along the base of the exterior walls. This method is not limited to cripple wall construction; it can also be used for a house built on a basement or slab-on-grade foundation or on another type of crawl space foundation.

Structural Protective Measures (Continued)

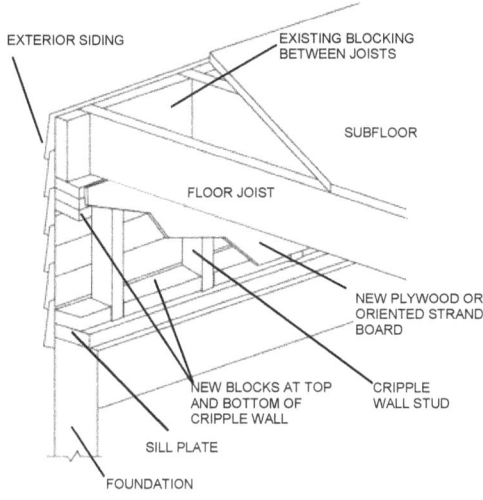

Figure 9. Bracing a Cripple Wall

Some houses are built on cripple walls. As shown in Figure 9, a cripple wall is a short wall that rests on the foundation and supports the floor and exterior walls. If the cripple wall is not braced, it can shift during an earthquake. When this occurs, there is a greater likelihood that your house will be severely damaged and that you and members of your family will be injured.

If your house is built on cripple walls, one way to increase its stability and reduce earthquake damage is to brace the cripple walls. In this method, horizontal blocking that consists of 2" x 4" boards is added between the vertical studs at the top and bottom of the cripple wall and, if necessary, at other locations between the studs. New vertical studs can also be added if necessary. Plywood or oriented strand board is then nailed to the interior face of the cripple wall. Also, nails are added through the existing blocking between floor joists to ensure that the floor is securely attached to the cripple wall.

Masonry chimneys pose a real hazard in earthquakes, especially the free-standing section above the roof line. To prevent the chimney from breaking away from the house, you may need to have it secured to the framing of the roof with sheet metal straps and angle bracing. Have the chimney inspected by a professional to determine the best method.

An indepth Homeowner's Guide to Earthquake Retrofit is available online at from the Institute for Business and Home Safety (www.ibhs.org/publications). This guide gives step-by-step illustrated instructions on how to complete both structural and nonstructural repairs, as well as pricing estimates and equipment lists.

Success Stories

Poulsbo, Washington

In late 1998, Doris Chapot purchased a two-story Cape Cod-style home built in 1902 that for years served as the First Lutheran Church parsonage. In 1940, the parsonage was moved to its present location. It was set on posts and concrete pier blocks, but nothing more was done to ensure its safety from earthquake damage.

At the time of purchase, a building inspector suggested that Chapot have an earthquake retrofit done to ensure positive connections among beams, posts, and pier blocks. Forty piers were braced with a gusset system that included a 2-foot, triangle-shaped plywood tying the posts to the concrete pier. All of the posts around the perimeter were tied together in the front and the back with 2-foot by 6-foot posts, and nails were strategically placed. Because pier blocks were different shapes, bendable metal connections were used for attaching the posts.

The retrofit project was completed on February 26, 2001. On February 28, a large 6.8 magnitude earthquake, with the epicenter located in the Nisqually basin in western Washington State, caused an estimated $2 billion in damages. Movement was felt as far north as Vancouver, British Columbia, and as far west as Salt Lake City, Utah.

Chapot was on the second floor during the earthquake. "I've been through many earthquakes during my lifetime and the house rode beautifully."

After a careful inspection under the house, not even a hint of damage was detected. "Not one thing in the house fell or broke! It feels so good to be safe!"

Success Stories (Continued)

Los Angeles, California

Anheuser-Busch operates a large brewery just a few miles from the epicenter of the January 17, 1994, Northridge Earthquake. The facility serves the company's markets throughout the Southwest and Pacific regions. Because it is in a high earthquake-hazard area, Anheuser-Busch initiated a risk reduction program at the brewery in the early 1980s.

A risk assessment of critical buildings and equipment was performed. Those with unacceptable levels of risk were seismically upgraded, without impacting daily operations.

Seismic reinforcements were designed for a number of buildings and the critical equipment contained within, including buildings housing beverage production and vats where the beer is stored and aged.

The Northridge Earthquake produced very strong ground motion, causing extensive damage in the immediate vicinity of the brewery. However, post-earthquake surveys conducted by the company's engineering consultants indicated that none of the retrofitted structures sustained damage. Onsite facilities of lesser importance to the business had not been strengthened and consequently sustained damage, requiring repairs. None of the vats, which are essential to the brewery's operations, were damaged. The brewery was quickly returned to nearly full operations following minor cleanup, repairs, and restoration of the offsite water supply.

Anheuser-Busch conservatively estimates that had seismic strengthening not been performed, direct and business interruption losses at the brewery could have exceeded $300 million. According to Anheuser-Busch, this is more than 15 times the actual cost of the loss control program.

Clearly, this loss control program paid for itself in the Northridge Earthquake event.

Summary: Key Steps To Protect Against Earthquake Damage

This lesson reviewed the following steps you can take to protect your home or business against earthquake damage.

- ☐ Secure heavy furniture and other items.
- ☐ Secure loose items and equipment.
- ☐ Fasten water heaters.
- ☐ Secure propane and fuel tanks.
- ☐ Anchor wood-burning and free-standing stoves.
- ☐ Bolt the sill plate of the building to the foundation.
- ☐ Brace cripple walls.
- ☐ Secure chimneys to roof framing.

The protective measures you consider depend on where your house or business is located.

Is your location at moderate to high risk of earthquakes? If so, decide which protective measures make the most sense in your situation, and take appropriate nonstructural and structural protective measures.

Earthquake Protection Resources

A number of resources offer indepth information that can help you learn more about particular earthquake protection options.

FEMA Resources

The following publications are available through the FEMA website at http://www.fema.gov/hazards/earthquakes/nehrp/home_school.shtm

- Avoiding Earthquake Damage: A Checklist for Homeowners
- Reduce Your Risk From Natural Disasters
- Earthquake Backgrounder
- Earthquake Fact Sheet
- How To Series: Protecting Your Property from Earthquake
- FEMA 74-Reducing the Risks of Nonstructural Earthquake Damage: A Practical Guide. Third Edition
- FEMA 232-Home Builder's Guide to Seismic Resistant Construction

For additional information on earthquakes and earthquake mitigation, consult:

National Earthquake Hazard Reduction Program Agencies

- National Institute of Standards and Technology (NIST) . http://www.nist.gov
- National Science Foundation (NSF) http://www.nsf.gov
- United States Geological Survey (USGS) http://www.usgs.gov
- USGS's Advanced National Seismic System (ANSS) http://www.anss.gov

Federal Partners

- National Aeronautics and Space Administration's (NASA) Earth Observatory http://earthobservatory.nasa.gov
- National Oceanic and Atmospheric Administration's (NOAA) West Coast and Alaska Tsunami Warning Center (WCATWC) http://wcatwc.arh.noaa.gov
- NOAA's National Tsunami Hazard Mitigation Program http://www.pmel.noaa.gov/tsunami-hazard

Regional Consortia

- Cascadia Region Earthquake Workgroup (CREW) http://www.crew.org
- Central United States Earthquake Consortium (CUSEC) http://www.cusec.org
- Northeast States Emergency Consortium (NESEC) http://www.serve.com/NESEC
- Western States Seismic Policy Council (WSSPC) http://www.wsspc.org

Lesson 5. Protecting Against Earthquake Damage

The questions below review key points about protecting your home or place of business from earthquake damage. After completing the questions, you can check your answers on the answer sheet located after the course glossary.

1. Earthquakes occur most frequently _____ of the Rocky Mountains.

2. Nonstructural measures to avoid earthquake damage include: (Mark all that apply.)

    ☐ Securing heavy furniture.

    ☐ Fastening water heaters.

    ☐ Elevating the structure.

    ☐ Securing propane and fuel tanks.

3. Identify three examples of kitchen or laundry equipment that should be securely anchored to the floor, wall, or countertop.

    _____

    _____

    _____

4. Select the protective measure on the right that would be used to protect the structure on the left, and write the appropriate letter on each blank space.

    ___ Sill plate   a. Bolt securely to the foundation

    ___ Cripple wall   b. Secure with sheet metal straps and angle bracing

    ___ Chimney   c. Brace with horizontal blocking

5. All 50 States and all U.S. territories are vulnerable to earthquakes.

    ___ True   ___ False

1 Percent Flood Level – The elevation of the maximum flood level with a one-percent chance of occurring within any given year, also known as the projected flood level. "A" zones, designated as Special Flood Hazard Areas (SFHAs) are at risk of flooding during the 1 percent flood.

Backflow Valve – Designed to block drainpipes temporarily and prevent flow into the house. Also called the "check valve," which allows water to flow in one direction (out of the house), but automatically closes when the direction of flow is reversed.

Base Flood – Flood that has a one percent probability of being equaled or exceeded in any given year. Also known as the 100-year flood.

Base Flood Elevation (BFE) – Elevation of the 100-year flood. This elevation is the basis of the insurance and floodplain management requirements of the National Flood Insurance Program.

Berm – Small levees, usually built from fill dirt.

Cladding – A layer of some metal or alloy bonded to another metal.

Coastal Flooding – The inundation of land areas along the oceanic coast that is caused by sea waters over and above normal tidal action. Such flooding can originate from the ocean front, back bays, sound, etc.

Crawlspace – Type of foundation in which the lowest floor of a house is suspended above the ground on continuous foundation walls.

Cripple Wall – A short wall that rests on the foundation and supports the floor and exterior walls of a structure.

Creosote – A black oily liquid with a pungent odor used as a wood preservative.

Debris – Materials (broken bits and pieces of wood, stone, glass, etc.) carried by wind or floodwaters, including objects of various sizes.

Disaster – Any natural catastrophe or, regardless of cause, any fire, flood, or explosion in any part of the United States which, in the determination of the President, causes damage of sufficient severity and magnitude to warrant major disaster assistance to supplement the efforts and available resources of States, local governments and disaster relief organizations in alleviating the damage, loss, hardship, or suffering caused thereby.

Dowel – A short cylinder of wood, metal, etc., usually fitted into corresponding holes in two pieces to fasten them together.

Downdraft – A sudden descent of a stream of cool air from above, often causing windshear.

Downdraft Furnace – A furnace with a downward air current.

Dry Floodproofing – Protecting a building by sealing its exterior walls to prevent the entry of flood waters.

Earthquake – A sudden, rapid shaking, sometimes violent, of the Earth caused by the breaking and shifting of rock beneath the Earth's surface.

Elevation – In retrofitting, the process of raising a house or other building so that it is above the height of a given flood.

El Niño – the phenomenon of a warm current replacing normally cool waters off the coast of Peru. Coastal winds usually push away surface water and the water is replaced by cold, nutrient-rich water from deep in the ocean, which supports abundant sea life. El Niño shifts the normal storm tracks of the U.S. farther north, producing a warmer than average winter in the Northwest and a wetter than average winter in the Southeast.

Emergency – Any hurricane, tornado, storm, flood, high water, wind-driven water, tidal wave, tsunami, earthquake, volcanic eruption, landslide, mudslide, snowstorm, drought, fire, explosion, or other catastrophe in any part of the United States which requires federal emergency assistance to supplement State and local efforts to save lives and protect property, public health and safety, or to avert or lessen the threat of disaster.

Epicenter – The area of the Earth's surface directly above the place of origin, or focus, of an earthquake.

Epoxy – Blended with other chemicals to form strong, hard chemically resistant substances used as adhesives, enamel coatings, etc.

Erosion – Process by which flood waters lower the ground surface in an area by removing upper layers of soil.

Federal Emergency Management Agency (FEMA) – Former independent agency that became part of the Department of Homeland Security in March 2003, tasked with responding to, planning for, recovering from, and mitigating against disasters. FEMA administers the National Flood Insurance Program.

Fill – Material such as soil, gravel, or stone which is dumped in an area to increase the ground elevation. Fill is usually placed in layers, with each layer compacted.

Flash Flood – Flood that rises very quickly, occurring suddenly, within a short time (from minutes to less than 6 hours), and usually is characterized by high flow velocities. Flash floods often result from intense rainfall over a small area, usually in areas of steep terrain.

Flood – Under the National Flood Insurance Program (NFIP), a partial or complete inundation of normally dry land areas from 1) the overland flow of a lake, river, stream, ditch, etc.; 2) the unusual and rapid accumulation or runoff of surface waters; and 3) mudflows or the sudden collapse of shoreline land.

Flood Elevation – Height of flood waters above an elevation datum plane.

Flood Insurance Rate Maps (FIRMS) – The official map of a community prepared by FEMA, showing base flood elevations along with the special hazard areas and the risk premium zones.

Floodplain – Any area susceptible to inundation by water from any source.

Floodproofing – Using materials and practices that will prevent or minimize flood damage in the future.

Floodwall – Flood barrier constructed of manmade materials, such as concrete or masonry.

Floodway – The channel of a river and the adjacent overbank areas reserved to carry base flood discharge without raising the BFE more than a designated amount

Fujita Tornado Scale – Usually referred to as the F-Scale, it classifies tornadoes based on the damage caused. It assigns categories as F-0 through F-5. It was developed by Dr. Theodore Fujita.

Hasp – Hinged metal fastening for a door, window, lid, etc., especially a metal piece that fits over a staple and is held in place by a pin or padlock.

Hazard Identification – A review of hazards, and of locations and conditions associated with hazards in a particular area; being aware of those hazards which, if they occur, could harm a community.

Human Intervention – Any action that a person must take to enable a flood protection measure to function as intended. This action must be taken every time flooding threatens.

Hurricane – A severe tropical disturbance in the North Atlantic Ocean, Caribbean Sea, or Gulf of Mexico that achieves a sustained wind force of a least 74 miles per hour.

Hurricane Straps – Usually galvanized metal, designed to help hold your roof to the walls, reducing the risk of losing your roof to high winds.

Hydrodynamic Force – Force extended by moving water.

Hydrostatic Force – Force exerted by water at rest, including lateral pressure on walls and uplift (buoyancy) on floors.

Joists – Any of the parallel planks or beams that hold up the planks of a floor or the ceiling.

Levee – Flood barrier constructed of compacted soil.

Mitigation – Sustained actions taken to reduce or eliminate long-term risk to people and property from hazards and their effects.

Mudflows – Sometimes called debris flows, are rivers of rock, Earth, and debris saturated with water. They develop when water accumulates rapidly in the ground, so that the Earth becomes a flowing river of mud (called a *slurry*).

National Flood Insurance Program (NFIP) – Provides the availability of flood insurance in exchange for the adoption and enforcement of a minimum local floodplain management ordinance. The ordinance regulates new and substantially damaged or improved development in identified flood hazard areas.

Ocean Flooding – Flooding caused by storm surge and wave action and affects primarily coastal areas, especially those along the beachfront.

Plate Tectonics – Theory that the Earth's surface is made up of about ten large plates and a number of small ones that fit together like a jigsaw puzzle. Plates are constantly moving, though slowly. When the stress exceeds the strength of the rock, the rock ruptures --or breaks--along a pre-existing or new fracture plain known as a fault. When the rock ruptures, it causes the Earth to tremble.

Preparedness – Activities to ensure that people are ready for disaster and respond to it effectively. Preparedness requires figuring out what will be done if essential services break down, developing a plan for contingencies, and practicing the plan.

Projected Flood Level – The elevation of the maximum flood level with a one-percent chance of occurring within any given year, also known as the one percent or 100-year flood.

Relocation – In retrofitting, the process of moving a house or other building to a new location outside the flood hazard area.

Reinforcement – Inclusion of steel bars in concrete members and structures to increase their strength. or other hazards.

Retrofitting – Making structural changes to an existing building to protect it from hazards such as flooding, high winds, and earthquakes. Retrofitting may range from simple measures to major construction.

Richter Scale – a measure of the amplitude of seismic waves. The scale is logarithmic, which means that an Earthquake that measures 7 on the Richter Scale has ground motion 10 times as large as one with a measurement of 6. Earthquakes of 6 or more are considered major. Extremely strong Earthquakes have magnitudes of 8 or more.

Riverine Flooding – Occurs when a river or stream flows over its banks and causes considerable inundation of nearby land and roads. Riverine flooding is a longer-term event that may last a week or more.

Saffir-Simpson Scale – A disaster-potential scale used by the National Oceanic and Atmosphere Administration's hurricane forecasters. The scale assigns storms to five categories. All hurricanes are dangerous but some are more so than others. The scale was designed to make comparisons easier and to make the predicted hazards of approaching hurricanes clearer to emergency forces.

Scour – Process by which floodwaters remove soil around objects that obstruct flow, such as the foundation walls of a house.

Sealant – In retrofitting, a waterproofing material or substance used to prevent the infiltration of floodwaters.

Seismic – Of, subject to, or caused by an Earthquake or an Earth vibration.

Seismic Event – The abrupt release of energy in the Earth's crust (the solid, rocky part of the Earth) causing an Earth vibration or Earthquake.

Seismograph – Used by scientists to record the changing intensity of the vibrations of an Earthquake.

Service Equipment – In retrofitting, the utility systems, heating and cooling systems, and large appliances in a house.

Sill Plate – A heavy, horizontal timber or line of masonry supporting a house wall, which sits directly on top of the foundation wall.

Slab-on-grade – Type of foundation in which the lowest floor of the house is formed by a concrete slab that sits directly on the ground. The slab may be supported by independent footings or integral grade beams.

Soffit – The horizontal underside of an eave.

Special Flood Hazard Area (SFHA) – Portion of the floodplain subject to inundation of the base flood, designated Zone A, AE, A1-A30, AH, AO, V, V1-V30, or M on a flood insurance rate map.

Storm Surge – Rise in the level of the ocean that results from the decrease in atmospheric pressure associated with hurricanes and other storms

Subgrade – Below the level of the ground surface.

Sump Pump – Device used to remove water from seepage or rainfall that collects in areas protected by a levee, floodwall, or dry floodproofing. In addition, a sump pump is often part of a standard house drainage system that removes water that collects below a basement slab floor.

Tornado – The most violent storms on Earth, with estimated wind speeds of 250 mph or more. At tornado is a violently rotating column of air extending between a cloud (often a thunderstorm loud) and the ground. The spinning motion of a tornado is almost always counterclockwise. Thunderstorms, nicknamed "twisters, develop in warm, most air in advance of eastward-moving fronts. A **funnel cloud** is a similar column of air that is not in contact with the ground. A **water spout** is a tornado that is over water. When either a funnel cloud or a water spout come in contact with the ground, they become, by definition, a tornado.

Truss – A rigid framework of beams, girders, struts, bars, etc., for supporting a roof, bridge, etc.

Tsunami – (pronounced soo-náh-mee) A series of ocean waves of extremely long length, generated by disturbances from Earthquakes, underwater volcanic eruptions, or landslides occurring below or near the ocean floor.

Veneer – Nonstructural, decorative, exterior layer of brick, stone, or concrete block added to the walls of a building, sealing all openings, including doors, to prevent the entry of water.

Vulnerability Analysis – Identifying how people, properties and structures will be damaged by a disastrous event.

Wet Floodproofing – Protecting a building by allowing flood waters to enter so that internal and external hydrostatic pressures are equalized. Usually only enclosed areas used for parking, storage, or building access are wet floodproofed.

Wildland-Urban Interface – The area where homes and structures meet the natural environment of forests and wildlands.

Wind – Air in motion parallel to the surface of the ground.

Windshear – A sudden variation in the vector of wind flow that is especially dangerous to aircraft during takeoff and landing.

Lesson 1. Overview: Protecting Against Disasters

1. The most common type of disaster in the United States is **flooding**.

2. This course will cover the following types of hazards that threaten your home or place of business. (Mark all that apply.)

   X Flooding

   __ Landslide

   X Earthquake

   X Tornado

   X Hurricane

   __ Tsunami

   X Wildfire

3. Write below two sources of local government information you can consult to learn about hazards that affect your area. (Any two of the following:)

   ▪ Building and zoning officials
   ▪ Planning department
   ▪ Floodplain manager
   ▪ Emergency manager

4. An example of a structural measure to protect against damage is to elevate a building in a flood-prone area.

   True

Lesson 2. Protecting Against Water Damage

1. A **flood map** of your community may show a projected flood level for your neighborhood or place of business.

2. Retrofitting measures to protect a structure against water damage include: (Mark all that apply.)

   X **Elevating utilities and service equipment.**
   X **Dry floodproofing.**
   __ Obtaining adequate flood insurance.
   X **Elevating the structure above the projected flood level.**

3. Write below two utilities that could be moved or elevated above the projected flood level. (Any two of the following.)

   ▪ Main electric switch box
   ▪ Electric outlet and switches
   ▪ Washer and dryer
   ▪ Furnace and water heater

4. Select the protective measure on the right that would be used to protect the item on the left, and write the appropriate letter on each blank space.

d	Floor drains	a. Install backflow valves
a	Sewer system	b. Anchor
b	Fuel tanks	c. Elevate
c	Washer and dryer	d. install float plugs

5. You can buy flood insurance even if you don't live or own a business in a flood hazard area.

   True

Lesson 3. Protecting Against Wind Damage

1. Hurricanes can be predicted, so you have 2 to 3 days to prepare, but **tornadoes** strike with little warning.

2. Mark any of the following structures that are especially susceptible to wind damage.

   ___ Brick houses

   X   One- and two-story wood-frame houses

   X   Manufactured homes

   ___ Steel-frame commercial buildings

3. Write below three protective, **nonstructural** measures you can take in the 24 hours before a hurricane is predicted to hit your area. (Any three of the following☺

   - Move breakable items away from doors and windows.
   - Board up doors and windows.
   - Bring in outdoor furniture and other personal property kept outdoors.
   - Secure manufactured home anchors.
   - Secure outbuildings.
   - Secure or move boats.
   - Turn off propane tanks.

4. Select the protective measure on the right that would be used to strengthen or protect the structure on the left, and write the appropriate letter on each blank space.

c	Roof	a.	Secure with sliding bolts
a	Double-entry doors	b.	Install horizontal bracing
b	Garage door	c.	Install hurricane straps
d	Window	d.	Buy or make storm shutters

5. Safe rooms built below ground level provide the greatest protection.

   True

Lesson 4. Protecting Against Wildfires

1. The most common type of wildfire is a surface fire, which generally is started by **people**.

2. Fire-resistant roofing materials include: (Mark all that apply.)

   X Tile roofing

   __ Asphalt shingles

   X Metal roofing

   __ Wood shakes

3. Identify three measures that can be used to create a safety zone around a home or place of business. (Any three of the following:)

   - Remove leaves and rubbish from under structures.
   - Thin a 15-foot space between tree crowns, and remove limbs within 15 feet of the ground.
   - Remove dead branches that extend over the roof.
   - Prune tree branches and shrubs within 15 feet of a stovepipe or chimney outlet.
   - Ask the power company to clear branches from powerlines.
   - Remove vines from the walls of the home.
   - Mow grass regularly.
   - Do not connect wooden fencing directly to your home.
   - Clear a 10-foot area around propane tanks and the barbecue and place a screen over the grill.
   - Regularly dispose of newspapers and rubbish.
   - Place stove, fireplace, and grill ashes in a metal bucket, soak in water for 2 days, then bury the cold ashes in mineral soil.
   - Store gasoline, oily rags, and other flammable materials in approved safety cans. Place cans in a safe location away from the base of buildings.
   - Stack firewood at least 100 feet away and uphill from the building. Clear combustible material within 20 feet.

4. Select the protective measure on the right that would be used to protect the structure on the left, and write the appropriate letter on each blank space.

a	Openings	a. Cover with mesh screening
b	Chimneys	b. Clean regularly
b	Gutters	
a	Barbeque grill	

5. States located east of the Mississippi River do not experience wildfires.

   False

Lesson 5. Protecting Against Earthquake Damage

1. Earthquakes occur most frequently **west** of the Rocky Mountains.

2. Nonstructural measures to avoid earthquake damage include: (Mark all that apply.)

    X Securing heavy furniture.

    X Fastening water heaters.

    __ Elevating the structure.

    X Securing propane and fuel tanks.

3. Identify three examples of kitchen or laundry equipment that should be securely anchored to the floor, wall, or countertop. (Any three of the following:)

    - Stoves and ovens.
    - Built-in and countertop microwave ovens.
    - Garbage compactors.
    - Dishwashers.
    - Refrigerators and freezers.
    - Clothes washers and dryers.
    - Ironing equipment.

4. Select the protective measure on the right that would be used to protect the structure on the left, and write the appropriate letter on each blank space.

a	Sill plate	Bolt secured to the foundation
c	Cripple wall	Secure with sheet metal straps and angle bracing
b	Chimney	Brace with horizontal blocking

5. All 50 States and all U.S. territories are vulnerable to earthquakes.

    True

Reminder . . .

It is now time to take the final examination. To take the final examination, log on to
http://training.fema.gov/EMIWeb/IS/ and follow the links for *Protecting Your Home or
Small Business From Disasters, IS 394.A.*